AF243966

Sin Revisited

Sin Revisited

by

Solange Hertz

Arcadia
MMXV

The writing in this volume spans nearly a quarter of a century. Part One was published privately in 1975 under the title *Sin Revisited,* with the exception of the postscript on "Devil Fighting," which made its first appearance in the pages of Immaculata magazine and was subsequently included in *Notebook on the Devil and Exorcism,* a paperback published by Marytown Press in 1974. Part Two is of recent vintage, some of it compiled from notes made over the years, some of it penned only now. If the style throughout the text lacks uniformity, that is the reason. Twenty-five years is a long time here below, and for better or worse, scribblers change like everyone else.

God knows, "My doctrine is not mine!" (John 7:16). I only hope that in these dreadful times which are His will for us, readers may find this "vulgarization" of the teaching of some of the greatest masters of the spiritual life a clear and present help in tribulation.

Solange Strong Hertz
Big Rock, Leesburg, Virginia
September 30, 1995
Birthday into eternity of St. Thèrese, the Little Flower of Carmel

Table of Contents

Introduction...1

Gluttony...9

Lust...19

Greed..32

Anger..41

Depression 52

Boredom 60

Vanity 68

Pride 77

Postscript 87

Revisiting Sin with St. John of the Cross..........92

Pride 96

Avarice... 101

Lust.. 105

Anger 111

Gluttony 114

Envy 119

Sloth 123

The Deadly Desires 127

The Devil Revisited 135

Bibliography 143

Introduction

What is so delicious as hurling a well-chosen epithet at the idiot who just backed into your petunias? What can equal three helpings of *marrons glacés?* Or another fistful of peanuts? Or fornication, especially if you feel it develops your personality?

The trouble with sin is it feels so good. It seems to fill a real need. If it didn't, who would bother with it? I've done a lot of thinking about sin here at the house, and I've decided to write this book about it. I expect a large reading public, because sin is one topic everybody knows something about first-hand. It's congenitally fascinating.

If you decide to read on, however, don't expect to find the seven deadly sources so familiar in song and story. You'll find eight, and even these won't be in the same sequence most of us are used to. This approach is newer than Vatican II, because it's so much older, if you know what I mean, very much older certainly than the old Baltimore Catechism.

As our Lord said, "Every scribe instructed in the kingdom of heaven is like to a man that is a householder, who bringeth forth out of his treasure new things and old" (Matt. 13:52).

Well, here's what I found.

Thomistic theology, based on Aristotle, gave us an excellent objective view of sin, classified under seven tidy headings based on reason. Reason tells us all sin is a form of pride, so that's where the list begins, progressing logically into the familiar avarice, lust, anger, gluttony, envy, before ultimately bogging down into sloth. This is eminently true and trustworthy, as the intellect sees sin, abstractly, and from a safe distance.

Please God I'll not fall into the sin of despising St. Thomas Aquinas, St. Gregory the Great or St. John of the Cross and St. Teresa, just to name a few doctors of the Church who used this classification with extraordinary results among all classes of people! This view will always be valid for those who approach their problems intellectually. And who doesn't at one time or another?

But there are different ways of looking at the same truth. Instead of looking down on sin from above, we can view it more "existentially," much as a housewife watches her good Sunday dinner become garbage as she scrapes the plates. Sin may be described, not as the intellect dissects it, but *as it happens* in any given individual.

There's nothing new to us about this humbler perspective. The Bible uses it almost exclusively. Our famous original sin in Eden, for instance, wasn't portrayed dispassionately as grand, primordial pride. It describes our first involvement with simple gluttony.

Of "the fruit of the tree which is in the midst of paradise," God had said, "we should not eat, and that we should not touch it, lest perhaps we die" (Gen. 3:3). God didn't say why. We had to take His word for it.

And gullible Mother Eve preferred to believe the serpent, who then as always, said there's really no such thing as sin. She saw very well for herself that "the tree was good to eat and fair to the eyes, and delightful to behold; and she took of the fruit thereof, and did eat."

And she gave her husband some.

Every infant begins the same way, through his stomach. And he does so as Adam did, through the agency of his "wife," his human body. There need be no apology, therefore, for taking the biblical approach to sin, in accordance with the earliest tradition of the Church.

Long before St. Thomas and the scholastics, the ancient Church Fathers described sin in no other terms than those the Bible uses. This was especially true of those stalwart easterners we call the Desert Fathers, who grappled nakedly with sin in the inexorable solitudes of the Egyptian Thebaid in the third and fourth centuries. Theirs was no flight into Egypt in the wake of the "infant" Christ, but a calculated foray into an arena where deadly combats between good and evil could take place at the most elemental level without mundane distractions. They were following, they tell us, the example of Christ grown to manhood, who was led by the Spirit for forty days into the desert to encounter the Enemy at close quarters.

The doughty "abbots" Serapion, Theodore, Cheremon, Joseph, Anthony, Paul, Isaac and their companions will be our guides in the pages that follow, God willing. They learned very much about sin in their solitary battles, and we would do well to listen to what they have to tell us about ourselves. They are quite in tune with the modern mind, for they are very much more "subjective" than St. Thomas or others nearer to us in time.

As a matter of fact, they were master psychologists in the true sense of the word, well aware of many principles which modern depth psychologists think they have discovered. Intensely practical, their interest in sin is anything but academic, recognizing it as a real and deadly disorder which must be cured at all costs.

They are concerned not so much with its "why" as its "how." They do not progress logically, but psychologically over devastated human topography, following one sin as it develops into the next as it does in real life, and not as it is treated in later ascetical textbooks. No godless analyst ever probed more deeply or ruthlessly into the human soul. Anyone truly interested in breaking himself of sin with God's help will find their pages fascinating. Others need not apply.

Every datum they left us bears the mark of bitter trial and error, but checked and counter-checked by the unfailing light of Holy Scripture given in answer to assiduous prayer. With this divine guidance they never fall into the lamentable aberrations which self-propelled secular psychology is so susceptible to .

Surprisingly enough, they don't begin their journey in Eden as we might expect. Their trek begins from Egypt, at a time when God's people have already long been held in the bondage of sin and slavery. They begin, in other words, with the real and existential situation of a sinner today, as he is found. They are not concerned with the—for us—purely academic falls of perfectly integrated individuals.

Egypt, they tell us, represents man's basic sin: *gluttony* Until Egypt and its fleshpots are left behind, we can never hope to enter the Promised Land and take on the seven hostile Canaanite nations that lie in wait for us there. These seven represent the other capital sins, whose opposition is determined and deadly, who resist being dislodged and often rise again after defeat. These must eventually be entirely exterminated.

But "thou shalt not abhor the Egyptian, because thou wast a stranger in his land" (Deut. 23:7). Thus Scripture teaches that we can't hope to destroy gluttony entirely like the other seven, because food is necessary to us and our very gluttony has been a means of supporting our life, even as Egypt for generations supported the Israelites. We always take something of Egypt with us. The Abbot Serapion compares the Christian with the eagle, who though he customarily soars above the clouds, must descend to earth periodically to feed on carrion to fill his belly. The best we can do with gluttony is check its incentives and superfluous cravings by the power of the mind.

Gluttony springs entirely from within us, needing no outside help. The other seven sins, however, take their occasion from outside us and must be destroyed totally and replaced by their opposites, just as the Israelites conquered and displaced the seven nations of Canaan. Nor were these peoples displaced unjustly, because they were usurpers, sons of Ham, who had first dispossessed the chosen sons of Sem to whom the land originally belonged.

Here is typified very important doctrine, which must be grasped at the outset of any serious study of sin, namely that *vice is not natural to us.* If it seems so, this is only because fallen nature is the only kind of nature we have ever known. God himself had to become man to show us what true human nature is, arriving in our midst through an immaculately conceived woman. Except for these two models, we have no firsthand data whatever on pure, integrated human nature.

Judging by fallen nature alone—as secular psychiatry must, for instance—we are bound to fall into disastrous miscalculations, both theological and practical. Ultimately we accept as "normal" whatever the majority of us happen to be doing at the moment, driving us headlong into immorality by majority vote, situation ethics and endless ramifications of perverted judgment.

There are no Calvinistic tendencies among the Desert Fathers. They are ruthless and realistic, but confirmed optimists when it comes to believing in man's essential goodness. Like all great masters of the spiritual life, they envisioned its progress and difficulties entirely in terms of the gradual restoration of the divine image in which man was created and which is his by right.

Because virtue is natural to us, asceticism destroys only what is necessary in order to restore us to our original condition. As our Lord said, "From the beginning it was not so" (Matt. 19:8). Perfecting human nature doesn't lie in adjusting to the Egyptian environment we were unfortunately born into. True human nature is the glorious Promised Land we hope to settle down in after all the interlopers are driven out.

Exposing to view the symbolism hidden in the Book of Joshua, the Fathers tell us that the seven nations Joshua fought successively in Canaan actually represent lust, avarice, anger, depression, boredom, vainglory and pride—in that order. We note with amazement that the envy and sloth we're used to hearing about don't figure in the list at all. That doesn't mean they aren't there, but in this "psychological" classification, we have to look for envy lurking in the territory between avarice and depression. Sloth belongs both to depression and boredom. We may not have looked at them this way before, but envy and sloth are really pretty much intellectual concepts, abstracted from what really goes on inside us.

Vainglory, on the other hand, is given an area all its own, whereas the scholastics preferred to regard it as simply a corollary of pride. And we note that the Fathers conclude their list with pride, where the scholastics begin. In practice, pride, the ultimate rejection of God in favor of self, is the final end of human sinfulness. Only a purely spiritual being like the devil can be capable of it straight off!

The sequence in which these sins occur tells even more about human frailty. Our initial gluttony is naturally followed by *lust* unless checked, for undue partaking of food normally leads to undue partaking of persons. After eating the forbidden fruit Adam and Eve realized immediately that they were naked. Lust in turn ushers in *avarice* or covetousness, for the shame it engenders impels us to hide behind extraneous possessions. We seek the covering of things, just as Adam and Eve sought loincloths and hid among the "trees of the garden" hoping to escape God's eye.

Doesn't everyday experience teach essentially the same thing, that we tend to rely on what we have to cover up what we are—or are not? Isn't this the underlying rationale of status-seeking? It springs, it would seem, from lust (whether conscious or un-admitted makes little difference), nourished by an inferiority complex caused by nothing more complicated than true guilt.

Anger soon follows, next in order. Covetousness automatically generates it when we can't have what we want. Modern psychology calls this "frustration" and thinks it has discovered something new when it postulates that it produces feelings of hostility. We're also informed that anger produces depression. But here again the Fathers got there first. *Depression* is next on their list after anger, figuring as number five of the eight principal sins. Wonder of wonders, have we ever thought of this complaint as *sinful*?

That depression indulged in is sinful becomes evident when we learn that it brings forth the next capital sin, boredom. That boredom is sinful is an even greater surprise. Obviously we'll have to overhaul our thinking drastically if we're to recover the scriptural direction on sin. Not only does it bypass scholastic notions, but it runs counter to many unchallenged professional dogmas. Try telling this to an analyst!

It follows, of course, that to overcome any one sin radically, the preceding one must be tackled. It's rather fascinating, when you come to think about it. Controlling temper, for instance, by searching into the hidden roots of avarice could well lead into chartless psychic territory not explored for about a thousand years. There are roads, but they're not new, and sadly overgrown. Returning to origins can be very hard going, but it's indispensable for a fresh start in all the directions this subject can take us.

So far the sins mentioned are closely related, leading one into the other inexorably unless checked forcibly at some point. Also, they require the cooperation of the body. The last two, *vainglory* and *pride*, are in a class by themselves, because they can be entirely spiritual, and they rise all the stronger and more vigorous after the others are conquered, glorying in all one's past victories.

"When thy enemy shall fall, be not glad, and in his ruin let not thy heart rejoice, lest the Lord see, and it displease him, and he turn away his wrath from him," warns Proverbs (24:17-18). Pride, alas, is the "sin of the perfect." It's the last to go.

After we leave the gluttony of Egypt, our enemies in the Promised Land are seven, but Scripture also calls them many, because each has its allies and satellites, its guerillas and undercover agents, its sympathizers and camp followers. We are troubled by them all, but each of us has a dominant opponent, more powerful against us than the rest, given our particular physiognomy and situation, demanding to be tackled first.

"Without me you can do nothing," God tells us (John 15:5). The Desert Fathers never tire of stressing this fact of life.

When the Lord thy God shall have brought thee into the land, which thou art going in to possess, and shall have destroyed many nations before thee, the Hethite, and the Gergezite, and the Amorrhite, and the Canaanite, and the Pherezite, and the Hevite, and the Jebusite, seven nations much more numerous than thou art, and stronger than thou:

And the Lord thy God shall have delivered them to thee, thou shalt utterly destroy them. Thou shalt make no league with them, nor show mercy to them: Neither shalt thou make marriages with them. Thou shalt not give thy daughter to his son, nor take his daughter for thy son ... Because thou art a holy people to the Lord thy God ...

Thou shalt not fear them, because the Lord thy God is in the midst of thee, a God mighty and terrible: He will consume these nations in thy sight by little and little and by degrees. Thou wilt not be able to destroy them altogether: lest perhaps the beasts of the earth should increase upon thee. But the Lord thy God shall deliver them in thy sight: and shall slay them until they be utterly destroyed (Deut. 7:1-6; 21-23).

If God is for us, and we obey His commands, who can be against us?

All we have to do is fight. This book is a field manual. It doesn't pretend to explore the "mystery of iniquity" at its deepest roots. Man's heart, Scripture tells us, is unsearchable. God alone can probe it, the false claims of modern psychology notwithstanding.

All we need to know God has told us already: that our irrational and indefensible proneness to sin lies in a *failure of faith,* just as Mother Eve's did.

At the suggestion of the serpent, she permitted herself to doubt God's word. Did He *really* mean exactly what He said about not eating the fruit? Wasn't there, after all, a more *adult* approach to the problem? Is there actually such a thing as sin? Isn't it, after all, more like a momentary snag in our inevitable evolution towards our omega point? Doesn't our liberation from Egypt set us free from old Judaic taboos?

There is no adult approach to sin. We proclaim our puling immaturity every time we fall into it. This book, please God, will not be such an approach. It's for infants in the spiritual life, but believing infants who take God at His word. He alone can save us from our sins, let alone forgive them; but as St. Augustine said, although He created you without your cooperation, He won't save you without it.

So here is some of Mother Church's most venerable advice on how to go about cooperating, pulled out of her vast storeroom. Here is what we must do with God's help in our frantic forays into Canaan. It's not spectacular work, but like any common foot-soldier's, it's essential if you want to win, or just stay alive.

Now, before preparing to leave Egypt, shall we take a last dispassionate look at what we're leaving behind?

Let's evaluate ...

Gluttony

What, exactly, makes it so finger-lickin' good? God knows. He made us for eating, and to make sure we wouldn't forget and starve to death, He attached considerable pleasure to it. For us, to be is to eat.

I eat, therefore I am.

Eating is part of creaturehood. Not self-sufficient, we can't exist at all without constantly partaking of something outside ourselves, even if it's only air. Our dependence on our Creator is total and eternal.

Everything God provides for us is "food" in the large sense. As our Lord told the devil, "Not in bread alone does man live, but in every word that proceedeth from the mouth of God" (Matt. 4:4). To His disciples He says, "My meat is to do the will of him that sent me, that I may perfect his work" (John 4:34).

Assimilating anything without reference to the divine will, just because we want to, is, strictly speaking, *gluttony.*

That the fall of mankind was strictly from hunger is historical fact. Mother Eve was the first woman who couldn't stick to a prescribed diet, because she was the first woman.

Gluttony is a life-long threat with us because we have to eat, and we have all inherited her basic weakness.

There's a hunger for everything. Eve was made to love good things, and she saw very well that the forbidden fruit was not only "good to eat" and sensually gratifying, but also "fair to the eyes," and "delightful to behold," for the knowledge it could give. Some people would rather gorge their eyes than their stomachs. Often they do both. (There is, after all, a theological reason for eating popcorn at movies or eating dinner in front of television.) Others avidly pursue knowledge, voraciously devouring books or graduate courses, or maybe battening on "dialogue." Still others hunger for praise or "beautiful experiences." Among the more spiritual, there's even a hunger for the yummy consolations to be found in prayer.

From the perspective of Eden, all sin can be seen as a crescendo of "gluttonies." It wasn't Sigmund Freud who discovered the pleasure principle as a motive for human behavior!

The elaborate Mosaic dietary laws, which we judge so arbitrary and materialistic today, were in fact designed to portray sin precisely in this way. When God forbade his chosen people to eat swine's flesh or geckos, He was teaching them they must not absorb into themselves just anything they pleased.

Obviously the sin didn't lie in succulent pork chops or noisy little reptiles; it lay in "eating" the evils these represent, and which God forbids. It lay in disobedience. In their true sense, the old Mosaic laws are as binding upon us as they ever were. As our Lord promised, not one jot or tittle of their content will be done away with, but only perfected and revealed in their true spiritual meaning.

The control of gluttony is therefore the key to the whole spiritual life. Popular modern psychology sees clearly enough that:

> Feeding is, unquestionably, the prime feature of daily life from the very first day of existence ... A baby is quite a tyrant; almost from the time of birth he learns that his mouth is a prime weapon in commanding the world as he knows it. Because howling and

crying bring him prompt gratification of his drives and desires, he has a sound reason for holding the oral cavity in high esteem. Such a baby, if all his whims are satisfied by an overanxious mother, goes on in life, continuing to pamper his mouth, eating well, depending on oral satisfaction to allay frustration. He may turn up in later life as the glib talker, the high-pressure salesman, teacher, actor or executive, etc. (James A. Brussel, M.D., *The Layman's Guide To Psychiatry*).

The same baby, psychiatry also tells us, soon finds he can also use his mouth to *bite*, not just his food, but others, as soon as he gets teeth. (The shortcut from gluttony to murder can be taken before we ever leave our cribs.)

Scripture told us all this long ago. To the Desert Fathers it was as plain as day that because we come into the world as nursing infants with an insatiable desire to absorb good things, the end of hunger for us can be nothing less than God. Because nothing else can really satisfy us completely, gluttony consists precisely in trying to find full satisfaction elsewhere. This is what makes it so dangerous. It can throw us off course radically, as it did Adam and Eve, right there in the beginning. Our whole life can degenerate into little more than a series of bites and chews.

The believer who at mealtime asks God to "Bless us and these Thy gifts," is not only taking cognizance of all the good things God has provided for us, and which He means for us to enjoy; but more important, he is asking God's help in assimilating them rightly, "blessing" those at table as well as the food. He is furthermore pronouncing a mild exorcism against the malefices of the Enemy, who can sometimes effect possession of his victim by ingestion.

Mealtime is a solemn occasion, properly accompanied by prayer, for God chose to become Food for us, even in this life. After the Last Supper, the most insignificant morsel should be recognized not only as a manifestation of everything God gives, but as a symbol and pledge of eternal life, of God himself.

It was for this that we were given stomachs, both carnal and spiritual, and not for the incidental pleasures of the palate. As never before it behooves us not to be gluttons. St. John of the

Cross, mystical Doctor of the Church, warns that we risk falling into this deadly vice even as regards the Eucharist, "being more eager to eat than to eat cleanly and perfectly."

Preparation for the Eucharist, as the Church has always taught, should begin where life begins, at the natural and physical level. The Fathers laughed at beginners who set themselves to controlling their thoughts without first acquiring some control of their stomachs, hoping to tangle with powerful Canaanites before they had even eluded the pursuing Egyptians. "It is impossible," reports John Cassian, "for a full belly to make trial of the combat of the inner man: nor is he worthy to be tried in harder battles who can be overcome in a slight skirmish!"

The Fathers discerned three forms of gluttony:

1. The first one consists in eating whenever we please. This might mean often or seldom, ahead of time or later, never or simply constantly nibbling between meals. Habitually indulged in, this form of gluttony quite predictably disposes its victim to restlessness and dissatisfaction with His state in life. It feeds instability.

2. The second form is being choosy about what we eat. In the world this might win us an international reputation as a gourmet, or simply as a weight-watcher, depending on whether our eye is on the menu or the calories, in other words, whether we are motivated by sensuality or vanity. There is no more refined form of gluttony than dieting from motives of pride. The dazzling authority on haute cuisine could fall into this category, but so might also the dear little old lady who insists on turning the host's kitchen upside down looking for a piece of dry toast, or the health fanatic who will consume only roots, berries and spring water. It's hardly surprising that this particular type of gluttony especially breeds covetousness, because its victims are orientated always to looking for something they haven't got at the moment. It's directly opposed to the perfect abnegation of

Christ, who told His disciples to "Eat such things as are set before you" (Luke 10:9).

3. The third type of gluttony is usually the one we think of as gluttony proper: eating as much as we want. Its victims are more likely to be fat, I suppose, and therefore more in evidence. Because there's a limit to what the stomach will hold, the Fathers tell us this one by a kind of inner necessity leads most directly into lust and sexual impurity, the next capital vice after gluttony. They were fond of quoting the prophet Ezechiel, who revealed that Sodom fell into the unbridled license with which her name became synonymous as a result of "fullness of bread and abundance" (16:49). No one with eyes could fail to see the relation between the glutting affluence of modern society and the so-called sexual revolution .

Carnal gluttony could hardly be called deadly in itself except that it unlocks the door, as we have seen, to all the other sins of which we are capable. No vice so lays bare, right at the dinner table where all can see it, the proud independence of the human will, its resistance to order and restraint, its slavery to sensuality. How many parents now deploring the licentiousness of their children never thought to stifle it at its source by the simple expedient of teaching them to eat only what is set before them at proper times!

By subjecting the spirit to the mindless whims of the body, gluttony literally reverses the order of creation in the same way that Adam did when he "listened to his wife." Its effects reach far beyond obesity, alcoholism or stomach troubles, for "not only is drunkenness with wine wont to intoxicate the mind, but excess of all kinds of food makes it weak and uncertain, and robs it of all its power of pure and clear contemplation." It stops spiritual progress dead.

Unchecked, it eventually ushers in apostasy, say the Fathers. We see around us today those heretics and apostates whom St. Jude twice characterized as men "walking after their own lusts."

He too cited Sodom and Gomorrah, for disordered appetites inevitably end by craving intellectual falsehood for their "itching ears" in the same way their stomachs were allowed to crave the "strange flesh" fancied in Sodom. Gluttons for punishment? St. Paul calls them "the enemies of the cross of Christ, whose end is destruction; whose God is their belly; and whose glory is in their shame; who mind earthly things" (Phil. 3:18-19) .

What to do?

Although their advice applies to everyone, the Fathers never deal in vague generalities. They are very explicit about how to deal with gluttony. In accordance with the three forms of the vice, they lay down three appropriate rules to follow:

1. Eat only at designated times.
2. Eat what is set before you.
3. Always leave the table with room for more.

We must, in other words, maintain order, plainness and sparseness in eating. (Foods requiring long and careful preparation come in for a special anathema. Sorry, gourmets.)

Even so, mastering these principles isn't quite enough. Because our nature is disordered at the very root of being, *we must fast.* Because we sin with both body and soul, both must suffer and make reparation. As St. Paul put it, "I chastise my body and bring it under subjection, lest perhaps after preaching to others I myself should be rejected" (1 Cor. 9:27).

We can never feel safe when it comes to gluttony, no matter how far we have advanced spiritually. We are always like the Israelites in the desert, secretly longing for the delicious onions and stews left behind us in Egypt. We're only too ready to return to the secure slavery of a welfare state rather than to learn free dependence on the delicate manna God provides for us.

We have our Lord's word for it that fasting, furthermore, when joined with prayer, is the ultimate weapon against the devil. The first official act of His public ministry, we might say, was the example of prayer and fasting He gave us during His forty days in the desert, by which He outmaneuvered the Enemy. As we know, it was because of their deficiency in fasting and prayer that later His disciples found themselves unable to cast out the dumb spirit from the epileptic boy whose father had come to them for help.

Asked why His followers didn't fast like St. John the Baptist's, He answered in effect, "Don't worry, they will!" He only advised that it be kept secret, so as not to feed vanity and self-righteousness.

But what about my *health?*

It's funny, but the Desert Fathers never mention it. Personally, I like St. Teresa's advice on the subject: Forget it. As if the proverbial longevity in the more austere contemplative communities hadn't already proved the point, now even modern science tells us that reduction in food intake actually delays the aging process.

Saints generally have concluded that health is either suffered or enjoyed, depending on God's will in particular cases. It's not their problem at all, but His. Whoever can't leave such worries behind is far from leaving all things for Christ, who positively forbade us to worry about food at all.

This doesn't mean that the Fathers were ignorant about particular foods and their effects. In fact, they probably knew very much more about them than we do. They counsel, for instance, to stay away from those which kindle lust. Unfortunately they neglect to tell us which these are, no doubt assuming that anybody knows these basics. Alas, how could they foresee how much our civilization would have forgotten once it discovered—and over-ate—on science!

They lay down no more definite rules for fasting than our Lord did, because none can be universally applied. Dealing as it does with material bodies, differences in age, sex and physical constitution must always be taken into account. Hard fasting for one individual could be feasting for another. In our own day

Mother Church leaves this delicate question very much to each one's conscience, although she never ceases to recommend abstinence from food as a basic means of maintaining spiritual balance and sharpening inner vision.

The Lenten liturgy implores "that our fasting may have a salutary effect, so that the mortification inflicted upon our body may benefit our souls" *(Collect,* Sat. after Second Sun.); and "that thy faithful who to mortify the flesh abstain from food, may likewise refrain from sin by the practice of justice." *(Collect,* Mon. after Second Sun.)

The end of fasting, after all, isn't gnawing hunger pangs, or even a beautiful figure, but joy and purity of heart. Without religious motivation, fasting soon degenerates into mere dieting or a display of ascetic prowess with purely natural rewards. Keeping the proper spiritual ends in view, too severe fasting can never be recommended (barring some special inspiration from God). In practice it drives us screaming and complaining back to Egypt for many unnecessary relaxations, and keeps us bouncing from feast to famine by turns. It's much more effective, and much harder, to practice dogged moderation in our fasts.

Also, because our Lord approved of His followers not fasting "as long as the bridegroom is with them" (Matt. 9:15), the Fathers tell us not to scruple about breaking voluntary fasts on social occasions. At such times, they maintain, Christ is present in the person of our guest and "mourning" is out of place. Not that social life can ever be used as an excuse for laxity. John Cassian, visiting in the desert of Skete, tells this story of himself:

> When one of the elders was pressing me to eat a little more as I was taking refreshment, and I said that I could not, he replied, "I have already laid my table six times for different brethren who had arrived, and pressing each of them, I partook of food with him and am still hungry, and do you, who now partake of refreshment for the first time, say that you cannot eat any more?"

Even at best, however, bodily fasting will avail us little if it's not accompanied by rigorous spiritual fasting, and in this regard we can be as ruthless as we please. Didn't our Lord tell us plainly that it isn't what goes into a man that defiles him, but what comes out of him? "For from the heart come forth evil thoughts, murders, adulteries, fornications, thefts, false testimonies, blasphemies" (Matt. 15:19).

Hear those super-psychologists the Desert Fathers on "soul-food":

> And let us not believe that external fast from visible food alone can possibly be sufficient for perfection of heart and body unless with it there has also been united a fast of the soul. For the soul has its foods which are harmful ... Slander is its food, and indeed one that is very dear to it. A burst of anger also is its food, even if it be a very slight one; yet supplying it with miserable food for an hour, and destroying it as well with its deadly savor. Envy is a food of the mind, corrupting it with its poisonous juices and never ceasing to make it wretched and miserable at the prosperity and success of another.

> Vainglory is its food, which gratifies it with a delicious meal for a time; but afterwards strips it clear and bare of all virtue ... All lust and shifty wanderings of heart are a sort of food for the soul, nourishing it on harmful meats, but leaving it afterwards without share of the heavenly bread and of really solid food. If then with all the powers we have, we abstain from these in a most holy fast, our observance of the bodily fast will be both useful and profitable. For labor of the flesh, when joined with contrition of the spirit, will produce a sacrifice which is most acceptable to God.

So much for fasting, necessary and efficacious. There is nevertheless, the Fathers say, only one real remedy for gluttony: *Anchoring the mind in the contemplation of divine things.*

This is simply a fancy way of saying that we must gradually learn to feed on God, beginning now in time the "eating" to which we are destined in the Beatific Vision. If even physical love-making or a passion for work or study can leave us no time to eat when we are in its throes, think what an awakened appetite for God and the things of God could do!

Where our hunger for God is concerned, no measures need be taken to check unruly appetite. We were made for Him. As St. Bernard put it, the measure of loving God is to love Him without measure. In Him all gluttonies are swallowed up and all desires satisfied.

"O taste and see that the Lord is sweet!" (Ps. 33:9).

"I am the living bread which came down out of heaven. If any man eat of this bread he shall live forever" (John 6:51-52).

Fortifying ourselves with this thought as we tighten our belts on the march from Egypt, perhaps we might do well to do a little reconnoitering and get an idea of what lies in wait for us once we get into Canaan. After their first glimpse, Moses' scouts returned petrified with fear. Ahead of them, they reported, lies a land "which devoureth its inhabitants: the people, which we beheld, are of a tall stature. There we saw certain monsters of the sons of Enac, of the giant kind: in comparison of whom, we seemed like locusts!" (Num. 13:33-34).

At this the vast majority of the Israelites were for leaving well enough alone and returning to Egypt as quickly as possible. (Reasonable people always find sanctity unreasonable.) Only Moses and Aaron, Caleb and Joshua found the courage to stand their ground, insisting that the Promised Land was well worth the effort.

"If the Lord be favorable, he will bring us into it, and give us a land flowing with milk and honey." As for its present inhabitants, "We are able to eat them up as bread!" cried Joshua and Caleb. "All aid is gone from them: the Lord is with us" (Num. 14:8-9).

The "locusts" weren't so sure. Eventually only God's flaming anger drove them forward into open provocation of such powerful opponents. The first one to be dealt with was the

Hethite who held Jericho. He was a tall monster indeed, commonly called ...

Lust

Nothing becomes a necessity so quickly as luxury. And we needn't be surprised that *luxuria* is in fact the classical word for lust. Of all the usurpers in the Promised Land there's no bigger bully, no greater phony. This ubiquitous Hethite finds friends and flunkies everywhere, establishing himself in every comer of the country.

Contributing nothing to the economy, he has nevertheless persuaded almost everybody that his services are indispensable and must be subsidized. His partisans are so emotionally involved with him they find it impossible even to speak of him objectively, and unfortunately only his partisans seem to be able to command a hearing. He has been there a long time. The reprobate Esau "offended the mind" of his parents by marrying two of his daughters, and generations later King Solomon followed suit.

Hopelessly taken in by his most blatant impostures, modern psychology is of little or no help to the Israelite fresh from Egypt when it comes to dealing with lust. For all practical purposes, lust and sex are identical in the modern mind, which seems to have lost all ability to discern what is part of the human condition and what is in fact entrenched vice, first established in the deformations of original sin and the laxities of youth.

The commonest and most deep-seated aberrations are considered normal because they are common and deep-seated. We have hardly known anything else, ever. Already in the fourth century John Cassian was well aware of the almost total loss of human perspective as regards lust. He admits that he tailors to his readers the instruction he himself received from the Fathers, stating candidly that those who have never themselves experienced true purity would simply never believe what these spiritual giants taught.

The goals they describe would be condemned, says he, as patently unrealistic and downright impossible. He doesn't expect his audience to believe, for instance, that periodic wet dreams are not part of man's natural physical life. Even less does he expect them to believe that in due course of time, with God's help, they can be eliminated entirely. The norms of fallen human nature are universally accepted without argument because these are the only norms of which most of us have any concrete experience. A virtue which transcends these completely as does perfect chastity is bound to appear unreal, arguing as it does for unheard of integration of body and spirit.

Outside the context of a human nature disintegrated by sin, however, the prescriptions of Leviticus concerning seminal ejaculations in men and menstruation in women make no sense at all. We read, for instance, that "If anyone that is defiled shall eat of the flesh of the sacrifice of peace offerings, which is offered to the Lord, he shall be cut off from his people" (7:20). Such uncleanness could be incurred in various ways, even by touching a dead body. Another way was sexual impurity, even though it occurred involuntarily:

"The man from whom the seed of copulation goeth out, shall wash all his body with water and he shall be unclean until the evening ... The woman with whom he copulated shall be washed with water, and shall be unclean until the evening" (15:16-18). A menstruating woman is similarly unclean, defiling anyone touching her (15:19 ff.)

Here again, as with the pork chops and geckos referred to with regard to gluttony, these material prohibitions must be judged according to their true spiritual and pedagogical sense. As a result of original sin, the bodily flows in question are no longer under our control, but they *should be*. If the Mosaic regulations single them out for emphasis, it is to make us aware of our deep-seated inherited sexual impurity, which can now be righted and supplied for only by the Creator himself.

Wet dreams and menstruation are universal in mankind today only because sin is universal in mankind, its effects actualized in our very bodies. Properly ordered human beings operating in perfect harmony with God's designs would not require the physical relief of periodic discharges to correct imbalances. All bodily processes and secretions would be self-regulating. Unless released for reproduction by an express command of the human will, sperm and ova would remain in the body, where they belong as due components. We would, in other words, be integrated. Such was the bodily state of our Lord and the Blessed Virgin on earth, and to say otherwise is both heretical and blasphemous.

Seminal and menstrual discharges were pronounced unclean by the old Law, however, not only because they happened to be glaring evidence of our loss of psychic harmony, but for a yet more compelling reason: Such discharges are intrinsically anti-life. They are *contraceptive*. The menstruous woman is normally sterile. With men it's obvious that reproductive cells lost in discharge are automatically subverted from the use to which God intended them. Neither remaining in the body nor uniting to generate further life, they are "spilled upon the ground" (Gen. 38:9). That this "detestable thing" perpetrated voluntarily by Onan can also occur involuntarily only goes to prove how profound is the disruption of our autonomy. How can opponents of *Humanae vitae* answer this argument from the Old Testament?

Chastity is indeed the most "integrating" of the moral virtues, reserving even our powers of union to God alone. Abbot Cheremon knew it to be very rare. He used to say that those who even believe perfect bodily chastity possible in this life are as few as those who actually attain it.

To arrive at any clear notion of what lust really is, enormous prejudices, misconceptions and popular opinions must be ruthlessly examined and subsequently disregarded. Unfortunately in our day—as always—it's precisely those who have little if any knowledge of chastity who set themselves up as authorities on sex. Attributing their own excesses to natural necessity, they even dare ascribe their intemperance to God himself, who they say created them so. The first man to do this was the first man, who told God it was "the woman whom *Thou gavest me*" who caused him to eat the forbidden fruit. No better excuse has yet been invented.

The truth of the matter is, man finds his God-given sexual powers so extremely difficult to control after Adam's defection, he often chooses to ease the tension by taking refuge in blasphemy. He has to persuade himself that by divine ordinance the satisfactions of sex are as necessary to his well-being as the satisfactions of hunger.

They're not. Truth himself came to tell us so, by both word and example. (This might be a good place to discuss the celibacy of the clergy, but we won't) Given the intellectually and spiritually blinding power of lust, it is only the chaste who can take its proper measure, seeing it clearly for what it is: a deadly effect and further cause of alienation from God.

But who has the courage to listen to the chaste?

Theirs is a hard saying. Few will like it.

They stress the mysterious inner connection between lust and gluttony already mentioned. Unlike other sins, these two arise immediately from natural appetites, demanding consummation in our very flesh, where the overflow of gluttony automatically produces its companion.

Although temptations to lust are known to be the devil's classic weapons against desert solitaries, he never tempted our Lord to impurity during His forty day fast in the wilderness. The fact is he couldn't, and he knew it. Our Lord's perfect resistance to the first temptation—to gluttony—precluded all possibility of falling into impurity. Our Lord had already virtually reversed the sin of Adam. By refusing to turn stones into bread when He was in fact "very hungry" He not only showed that natural appetite is no excuse for gluttony, but He also barred all entrance to sexual sin, or any other sin requiring bodily cooperation.

As with gluttony, the Fathers discern three forms of lust:

1. *Fornication,* or lust as it occurs between man and woman. This can occur within marriage as well as out of it; marriage is not a license to sexual excesses. Needless to say all pre-marital and extra-marital sex is fornication, if not outright adultery.

2. *Impurity,* which includes self-abuse and every kind of unnatural sexual relations with members of the same sex, animals or objects whatever.

3. *Lust proper,* which resides primarily in thoughts and desires, always beginning there whether overtly expressed or not. Our Lord spoke of this kind when He taught that "whosoever shall look on a woman to lust after her, hath already committed adultery with her in his heart" (Matt. 5:28).

Abbot Cyrus of Alexandria, questioned as to the imagination of lust, had this comforting answer to give:

> If thou hast not these imaginings, thou art without hope: for if thou hast not the imagination thereof, thou hast the deed itself. For he who fights not in his mind against sin, nor gainsays it, sins in the flesh. And he who sins in the flesh, hath no trouble from the imagination thereof.

Like eating, sex has a specific, intense pleasure attached to it which is ordered to the preservation of life—in this case the life of the species rather than the individual. As with gluttony, lust therefore consists in seeking, either mentally or physically, the pleasure apart from the purpose God ordained it to serve, or seeking it primarily.

(Seen in this light, contraception can at best be given recognition as lust's common law wife. Although she has acquired a modicum of social standing *de facto,* apart from her paramour she has no standing whatever in the Promised Land. When he is eliminated, she disappears with him. We shall therefore simply ignore her as unproductive and irrelevant. The whore's a bore anyway.)

Let's concentrate on the real enemy, lust. We must study his habits if we hope to weaken him. (Alas, as the Fathers sadly admit, almost no one overcomes him entirely.)

Because gluttony and lust are so intimately rooted in the body and can make their demands felt even involuntarily through its agency, they can never be controlled by exclusively spiritual means. Anger, depression or covetousness, for instance can be fought by ruthlessly restraining our thoughts, but like gluttony, lust requires bodily retrenchment as well to get at the source of the trouble. Both soul and body must be corrected. Unlike gluttony, however, lust can be extirpated completely without the slightest damage to nature. Although solidly entrenched in the Promised Land, it doesn't belong there by right and performs no essential function for the individual.

The battle against lust requires rigorous mortification. Once and for all over-ruling his followers' cowardly pleas to be allowed to return to Egypt, the first thing Joshua did after crossing the Jordan into enemy territory was to "make knives of stone" wherewith he circumcised a second time "the children of Israel in the hill of the foreskins" (Josh. 5:2-3). He did so at God's express command. Only the truly determined can be counted on to attack Jericho, which must be taken at all costs. Its position is highly strategic, commanding the whole lower Jordan valley and three great passes into the interior. It is the oldest city in the world, and heavily fortified. Whoever doesn't get past it can never occupy the rich fields beyond.

How serious are we?

As St. Paul says, "Know you not that they that run in the race, all run indeed, but one receiveth the prize? So run that you may obtain! And everyone that striveth for the mastery, refraineth himself from all things" (1 Cor. 9:24-25). He too was aware of the close connection between eating and sex, for he goes on to quote Exodus where the Israelites wound up falling into idolatry because they "sat down to eat and drink, and rose up to play."

> Neither let us commit fornication, as some of them committed fornication, and there fell in one day three and twenty thousand ...

Now all these things happened to them in figure: and they are written for our correction, upon whom the ends of the world are come (1 Cor. 10:7-11).

Fasting from food, especially liquids, is basic training. "The chastity of the inner man," say the Fathers, "is known by his temperance." A young man asking one of them how it was the elder had never been harried by lust, was told, "Since the time I became a monk I have never given myself my fill of bread, nor of water, nor of sleep, and tormenting myself with appetite for these things whereby we are fed, I was not suffered to feel the stings of lust." Abbot Serapion says we must add also bodily penance vigils, exhausting physical labor and determined flight from occasions of sin.

When it comes to the other vices, we are often helped by frequent contact with others, who may retaliate or reprimand us when we provoke them, thereby purifying us by painful on-the-spot therapy. In these cases the offense itself produces its own chastisement, bringing us all the sooner to repentance and amendment. Not so with lust. This vice is best grappled with in solitary combat, caught isolated and off guard without support.

"Quiet and solitude," say the Fathers, "are very useful in fighting this particular disease, so that the sick spirit, less troubled by various images, can arrive at purer insight and expel the contagion more easily." Weak fighters especially afflicted by lust should avoid, if possible, even being reminded of it, advises Abbot John.

Naturally they were brought up sharply here by those who reminded them in no uncertain terms that many good people manage to remain continent in the very thick of the world's business. To these they retorted, then as now, "Oh, continence, that's easy!"

What they are talking about is *chastity*, something very different. These two virtues bear about the same relation to each other as do letter and spirit. Continence is largely material, and basically negative. As the word itself implies, it manages to contain itself, to hold itself in. As such it's certainly not to be despised. Like the letter, it's necessary and makes a good beginning, but it can't go far enough.

Chastity is a positive achievement, a virtue so exalted very few ever attain it, or even suspect its existence. The Fathers were of the opinion that it is rarely granted except to virgins in body as well as soul, as were the two Johns of the New Testament, or the prophet Elias, or Jeremias or Daniel, or some giants of penance and mortification.

In the final analysis, it is a special gift from God, unattainable by human effort supported by ordinary grace. It is tantamount to possessing human nature in its full, integral perfection. Only our Lord and his Blessed Mother have possessed it in its fullness. Trying to describe it is like trying to describe heaven, or any other bliss of which we have had no experience on earth.

St. Paul doesn't hesitate to equate chastity with sanctity:

> For this is the will of God: your sanctification; that you should abstain from fornication; That everyone of you should know how to possess his vessel in sanctification and honor: Not in the passion of lust, like the Gentiles that know not God ... The Lord is the avenger of all these things ... Therefore he that despiseth these things, despiseth not man, but God (1 Thess.4:3-8).

Abbot Cheremon distinguishes six progressive degrees in the acquisition of chastity:

The first is reached when we no longer succumb to temptations of the flesh during waking hours.

The second degree consists in never dwelling on the slightest voluptuous thought.

Third, when the sight of the opposite sex arouses not the slightest concupiscence.

Fourth, even innocent movements of the flesh are no longer experienced during the day.

In the fifth degree, discussing or reading about human generation elicits no greater emotional response—either at the time or in retrospect—than would dwelling on brick making or some other trade.

Those who reach the sixth degree are not troubled by voluptuous images even during sleep.

There is a higher degree yet, the Abbot tells us, possible but given to very few: complete disappearance of involuntary seminal emissions. (Women must adapt this doctrine as they can. Unfortunately, our abbots were all men and give no directives specifically for females in their writings.)

Although severe mortification is necessary to acquire chastity, it's not a virtue which is sustained by austerity of life, as one might think. It is preserved by the very love of its own beauty, and the delights engendered by its purity. Its true hallmark is *peace*.

Measured against chastity, lust stands out in its full vileness. Hear St. Paul:

> But fornication, and all uncleanness, or covetousness, let it not so much as be named among you, as becometh saints: Or obscenity, or foolish talking, or scurrility, which is to no purpose ... For know you this and understand, that no fornicator, or unclean, or covetous person (which is a serving of idols), hath inheritance in the kingdom of Christ and of God.
>
> Let no man deceive you with vain words," he continues. "For because of these things cometh the anger of God upon the children of unbelief. Be ye not therefore partakers with them (Eph. 5:3-8).

Our Lady told the children at Fatima that more people go to hell as a result of sins of the flesh than from any other cause. Certainly the extent that impurity can unbalance all thinking and bodily processes may be deduced from the current ills of our sick society, which demonstrate how diffused and ramified are the operations of the unbridled sex drive. Sexuality chronically infected with lust carries poison far afield.

Together with its mother gluttony, no vice is so opposed to clear vision as lust. The holy Abbot Theodore went so far as to counsel one wishing to acquire a knowledge of Scripture,

> ...not to spend his labor on the works of commentators, but rather to keep all the efforts of his mind and intentions of his heart set on purifying himself from carnal vices, for when these are driven out, at once the eyes of the heart, as if the veil of the passions were removed, will begin as it were naturally to gaze on the mysteries of Scripture.

He said furthermore that,

> ...great differences and mistakes among commentators arise because most of them, paying no sort of attention towards purifying the mind, rush into the work of interpreting the Scriptures, and in proportion to the density of impurity of their heart form opinions that are at variance ... to each other's and to the faith.

The source of the rampant errors in every area of human thought today, both in the world and in the Church, would be quickly spotted by Abbot Theodore! We noted in the last chapter the organic connection between sins of the flesh and formal heresy as discerned by St. Jude.

Given the welter of "media-massaging" to which we are all subjected today, it's evident that fasting must be constant and thorough, devoid of subterfuge. Custody of the senses should be our first line of defense.

The God who made us and knows our nature far better than we do told us that a man who looks at a woman lustfully has already committed adultery with her in his heart. We have His divine word for it that the sight of her is not so much an occasion of sin as it is an occasion of revealing the evil which has lain hidden all along in her beholder, not to mention in the woman herself, who may be deliberately provoking his attention.

As the Fathers wryly note, a disease isn't contracted at the moment it breaks out; it has had its customary incubation period. It's this "incubation" of lust that they counsel us to pay particular attention to, for it's then that lust can be most easily brought under control. We are warned that if we don't regulate our thoughts during the day, they will erupt in full strength during sleep.

The Fathers are so refreshing, the way they tear those comfortable wraps from what we like to consider our blameless (and therefore inviolate) "subconscious!" They must laugh heartily at the modern notion that what the subconscious does isn't imputable to us, simply because the poor thing has no morals, cavorts like an idiot, and won't do anything it's told anyway. The masquerades of disordered sex were known centuries before Freud, who as a matter of fact drew most of his psychoanalytic "theories" from rabbinical mysticism and the *Kabbala*.

The abbots in fact posit squarely that *we are directly responsible for anything we voluntarily allow to work its way into the subconscious through the senses in the course of the day.* We can imagine what short shrift they would give current theories on the so-called "therapeutic" value of pornography, not to mention the hypocrisies of sensitivity training, transcendental meditation, and the various "touch-touch" schools of psychology. They would soon remind us that of all our senses, the sense of touch must never be allowed to indulge itself at will. (I leave the reader to reconstruct what they might say about the touch-play at certain liturgical celebrations.)

Joined to fasting from food and drink and unseemly sights, sounds and palpitations, we must keep an inviolable custody of the heart. Abbot Cheremon says:

> The greater our progress in gentleness and patience, the greater our bodily purity; we become grounded in chastity to the extent that we have driven anger from us. For it's impossible to

avoid the rebellions of our flesh unless the commotions in our spirit are extinguished.

In support of this contention he quotes the beatitude, "Blessed are the meek, for they shall inherit the earth," explaining that the "earth" is our own body, over which only the humble and patient acquire perfect autonomy. And it takes much patience in the battle against lust, who has so many allies. The devil we are warned is assiduous in tempting us in proportion to the rewards of chastity, which are exceeding great, both in this life and the next.

Chastity is a master virtue which perfumes the whole moral person. It determines the boundaries of the personality, maintaining its sacred privacy against the intrusions of the world, besides regulating all legitimate outside contacts with the neighbor. No chaste person is a loose talker, exposing his deepest feelings to one and all, nor does he receive all confidences indiscriminately. The chastity of the body is meaningless without this deeper moral chastity, of which it is the sacramental sign.

Modern psychiatry is probably the greatest single force organized against chastity since the beginning of the world. Specifically ordered to penetration into the human soul, the "garden enclosed" reserved to God alone, it demands indecent exposure from its "patients" as the continuing price of every consultation. Until recent times, at least among the faithful, only a priest, an *alter Christus* strengthened and empowered by a special Sacrament to act in God's place, was permitted like the High Priest to enter the Holy of Holies which is the heart of a human person created in God's image. No one else had, or could be given, the right to pry for purposes of healing, any more than anyone had the right to expose himself to the profane gaze of a self-appointed practitioner:

"Or know you not," asks St. Paul, "that your members are the temple of the Holy Ghost, who is in you, whom you have from God; and you are not your own?" (1 Cor. 6:19).

Defenses collapsed with the invention of what is called the "psyche," and it is an invention, a euphemism with no objective existence in reality. It is a creation of the imagination whereby godless psychiatry, by supposedly working in an area governed by purely natural psychological laws, conceals the fact that it is actually operating on the soul, the forbidden territory where God allows only His priests to minister.

Pretending to integrate the personality according to natural laws all the while dissolving its moral integrity, psychiatry is actually chaotic in its effects. Ordered primarily to "adjusting" the patient comfortably to the world, it is intrinsically evil in that it places the natural above the supernatural, setting up carnal norms and procedures where only grace should command the operation, let alone make the diagnosis. No one may enter the sanctuary of another human soul without committing a grave sin against chastity—as does the psychiatrist who is not a priest, or who, being a priest, enters there by purely human methods for human ends. Such intimate trafficking, now commonplace even among Catholics, sins against chastity at its deepest level. By comparison rape, prostitution or other violations of the body are nothing .

The one infallible sign, say the Fathers, that we have become pure is that no illicit images occur to us even involuntarily during rest or sleep. In effect, they insist, "the quality of our thoughts," not to mention our actions, "negligently guarded during the day due to distractions, is tested in the quiet of the night." Nor do we begin to come close to the virtue of chastity, they inform us, until we truly realize from hard experience that we can acquire it only with God's strength exerted in our behalf.

The siege of Jericho went on for six days. The city fell on the seventh and last, but not as a result of Israel's military prowess. Its defenses yielded only to supernatural force, in a manner prescribed by God himself:

> And they went before the ark of the Lord walking and sounding the trumpets ... and they went round about the city the second day once, and returned into the camp. So they did six days.

But the seventh day, rising up early, they went about the city, as it was ordered, seven times. And when in the seventh going about the priests sounded with the trumpets, Josue said to all Israel: Shout: for the Lord hath delivered the city to you!

...So all the people making a shout, and the trumpets sounding, when the voice and the sound thundered in the ears of the multitude, the walls forthwith fell down: and every man went up by the place that was over against him: and they took the city, and killed all that were in it, man and woman, young and old. The oxen also and the sheep, and the asses, they slew with the edge of the sword (Joshua 6:13-16; 20-21).

The symbolism is clear. Falling as it did to "shouting" and priestly trumpet blowing, Jericho was destroyed not by arms primarily, but by force of *prayer*. Joshua thereupon swore an oath before God, which is symbolically a religious vow of chastity:

"Cursed be the man before the Lord, that shall raise up and build the city of Jericho. In his firstborn may he lay the foundation thereof, and in the last of his children set up its gates!" (6:26).

To stir up lust is to condemn human generation to death before God. Let him take this who can.

Especially as all this while, just outside Jericho the obscure but powerful Gergezite has been lurking. He is ...

Greed

The Israelites encountered him very shortly after Jericho's walls came tumbling down.

With victory in sight, Joshua laid the whole town under ban. Every living thing was killed, but "whatsoever gold or silver there shall be, or vessels of brass and iron, let it be consecrated to the Lord, laid up in his treasures." He warned the people to "beware ye lest you touch aught of those things that are forbidden, and you be guilty of transgression, and all the camp of Israel be under sin, and be troubled" (6:19,18).

Needless to say, this is just what happened. A man called Achan (a name meaning "trouble," incidentally), couldn't resist the sight of the wealth his sword had ripped open before his eyes. He later confessed,

> I saw among the spoils a scarlet garment exceeding good, and two hundred sicles of silver, and a golden rule of fifty sicles: and I coveted them and I took them away, and hid them in the ground in the midst of my tent, and the silver I covered with the earth that I dug up (7:21).

His sin was costly, for the whole army was subsequently routed at Hai, the next town they tried to take. Until Achan was discovered and put to death with his whole family—even to his oxen and donkeys and sheep—the nation could proceed no further, so effectively does greed block all spiritual progress until the obstacles it places before us are removed. "Neither can Israel stand before his enemies," the Lord warned, "because he is defiled with the anathema" (7:12). And Scripture adds, "All Israel stoned him." A cairn was raised over Achan and all his belongings, including the fateful robe and the gold and silver abstracted from Jericho.

"Thou shalt not covet."

Those were rough, unsentimental times, but the divine message remains the same. The Son of God, himself delivered to death by a man bewitched by thirty pieces of silver, asks us:

> For what doth it profit a man, if he gain the whole world, and suffer the loss of his own soul? (Matt. 16:26). If thou wilt be perfect, go sell what thou hast, and give to the poor, and thou shalt have treasure in heaven ... a rich man shall hardly enter into the kingdom of heaven (Matt. 19:21,23).

Even as lust predisposes us to greed, so does the desire for chastity demand poverty.

Unless freed of the attractions of Jericho, we can never withstand the strong coalitions that form against us in geometric proportion as we advance into enemy territory. Avarice ushers in a whole new dimension in the economy of sin.

Properly speaking, it's a vice not natural to man in the sense that its occasions do not arise from man's physical constitution as do gluttony and lust, although these last certainly predispose us to it. Because it seeks satisfaction in objects outside our bodies, it's fairly easy to control in its beginnings. Not only can we forego these in one fell swoop without the slightest danger to survival, we can even make life easier for ourselves thereby. This is the reason for the religious vow of poverty, perfect concomitant to the vow of chastity, consecrating everything to the Lord, "laying it up in His treasures" as it were.

According to St. Luke's account, covetousness was our Lord's second temptation in the desert. Unable to propose fornication as a result of Christ's perfect resistance to gluttony, the devil tried the next possibility. Aware that attractions lying beyond mere bodily satisfactions can arouse hungers that are capable of ushering in any kind of evil, he gave Him a view of "all the kingdoms of the world," suggesting, "All these will I give thee, if falling down thou wilt adore me" (Matt. 4:8-9).

So it is, we're told, that one of the surest signs of success against carnal temptations is the sudden onset of fiercer, more subtle inducements than we meet with ordinarily. As we know, our Lord vanquished this one by refusing even to consider the bait. His renunciation of the goods of this world was total.

Moses had prescribed that before engaging in battle all fighting men be asked, "What man is there that is fearful and faint-hearted? Let him go and return to his house, lest he make the hearts of his brethren to fear, as he himself is possessed with fear!" (Deut. 20:8). The Fathers, who didn't take half measures themselves, felt that partial renouncement of the goods of this world is worse than none, if only because lukewarm Christians are a danger to others.

They cite the example of Ananias and Sapphira, who in the beginnings of the Church sold a property according to the Lord's precept, but "by fraud kept back part of the price of the land ...

and bringing a certain part of it, laid it at the feet of the apostles," lying about the transaction. As St. Peter remarked to them, "Whilst it remained, did it not remain to thee? And after it was sold, was it not in thy power?" They died at his feet, for giving up only part of what they could have kept entirely without sin or deceit. "And there came great fear upon all the whole church, and upon all that heard these things," concludes Scripture (Acts 5:2-11).

Unfortunately, if strong measures aren't taken at the outset, avarice takes deep root in the heart and becomes the hardest of all the capital sins to eradicate. Other faults like gluttony, anger or vanity can be said to have some good by-products; they keep us alive, or they make us impatient with our lack of virtue, but covetousness does nothing but add to itself.

Then too, carnal appetites have physical limits beyond which they cannot indulge themselves, try as they will; but when these hungers are transmuted into greed for possessions, they are no longer bound by the body, and become insatiable. Proverbially known as "the lust of old men," greed ordinarily increases with age, supplanting youthful physical appetites as these decrease. Become indeed the root of all evil, it feeds on everything it sees.

Because it is rooted in the heart and not in the body, it never produces satiety. On the contrary, one satisfied desire engenders another, so that as wealth increases, the mania of covetousness increases with it like fire consuming everything in its path. Its victims become like the man in the Gospel driven to "pull down my barns and ... build greater; and into them ... gather all things that are grown to me, and my goods" (Luke 12:18). Because its "needs" are artificially excited at will, greed leads to chronic discontent. The end of the miser is misery.

Our affluent society has spread a panorama of greed and its effects across a large canvas. Madison Avenue need only show a color photograph of some superfluity to make us desire it, if not crave it as an outright necessity. We have polluted the atmosphere with waste products of unbridled greed, all the while suffocating in accessories. Far from being hailed as an evangelical counsel, poverty has become a capital crime and a breeder, we're told, of criminals. We war on poverty as an enemy, all the while greed directs the campaign.

True to form, the Fathers discern three kinds of avarice:

1. They describe the first as a reluctance to let go of whatever it is we possess. It ranges from a simple lack of generosity in sharing with others to open rebellion against financial misfortunes sent by God. Persons so affected tend more to hoarding than to acquiring. In the last stages, they can't even give to themselves, like the miser who dies of starvation in destitute surroundings, lying on a mattress stuffed with his life savings.

2. The second variety, or "Lot's wife" syndrome, leads us to regret what we have given away, sometimes attempting to regain it, or exact some return for it. It's avarice somehow lodged in the memory, but just as deadly as it proved to Lot's wife, who was eternally immobilized by it.

3. Finally there is what we consider avarice proper: the inordinate desire for what we don't possess, with increasing emphasis on the superfluous. (Most things are superfluous, there being only one thing necessary!) Whether we keep our eyes glued to ticker tapes or just can't resist "collecting," the malady is the same.

This last kind causes perpetual restlessness, as do lust and gluttony, but unfortunately avarice is more self-propelling. As our current environment proves, wealth can finance wandering of all kinds, and then supply excuses for more wandering. Perhaps the most easily recognized example is the garden variety compulsive shopper, who clogs highways and shopping centers forever chasing a bargain. If stores are closed or money short, window-shopping can be indulged in, propagating desires that will produce more restlessness.

Avarice becomes increasingly independent of authority—if only through financial independence—until finally it will submit to no discipline but its own. This is as true of the individual as it is of the financial interests which now rule the world. This private discipline, however, soon reveals itself as grinding slavery, harnessing its victim to compulsive work which allows him no relaxation whatever.

Noting the phenomenon in hapless monks, the Fathers depict it thus:

> And so he is driven about, and more and more inflamed with the love of his money, which when it is acquired, never allows a monk either to remain in a monastery or to live under the discipline of a rule. And when separating him like some wild beast from the rest of the herd, it has made him through want of companions an animal fit for prey, and caused him to be easily eaten up, as he is deprived of fellow lodgers, it forces him, who once thought it beneath him to perform the slight duties of the monastery, to labor without stopping night and day, through hope of gain; it suffers him to keep no services of prayer, no system of fasting, no rule of vigils; it does not allow him to fulfill the duties of seemly intercession, if only he can satisfy the madness of avarice, and supply his daily wants; inflaming the more the fire of covetousness, while believing that it will be extinguished by getting.

This description is easily transposed to the secular milieu, where husbands and fathers infected by avarice parading as virtue (call it "providing" or "getting ahead" or whatever), no longer have time to spend with their families or with God. The prevailing cancer of our society known as the working mother attests what profound sociological wounds greed can deal. Where time is money, who can afford to keep the Sabbath holy, or even enjoy himself? Or bring up children?

Say the Fathers, overcoming avarice doesn't proclaim virtue so much as being subjected to it proclaims our shame.

Our Lord said truly, "You cannot be the slave both of God and of money" (Matt. 6:24).

"Watch," said our Lord, "and be on your guard against avarice *of any kind,* for a man's life is not made secure by what he owns, even when he has more than he needs" (Luke 12: 15).

Here divine wisdom exposes for us the hidden connection between avarice and *insecurity,* which may well be the hallmark of our society. In its headlong rush into the welfare state, where material needs are supposedly guaranteed, it betrays the deep spiritual disease that afflicts it. The avaricious are easily convinced they are on the verge of ruin or imminent starvation, and the more they acquire, plan for the future or lay in supplies, the more insecure they grow, for avarice and insecurity mutually feed each other until their victims are totally sacrificed to their demands. Worry about health alone, about who will care for them in sickness or old age, can literally drive them into their graves by over-work or anxiety.

Our lack of security dates from Eden. It springs from nothing more complicated than guilt, the same guilt which caused our first parents to hide among the trees of the garden for fear of meeting God. Guilt quite rightly makes us feel inferior, and our sense of inferiority in turn drives us to seek status, to cover ourselves, our nakedness, with possessions in an attempt to improve the deplorable picture. We can always find excellent reasons for doing so. After all, denying ourselves the goods of this world when they are available, we're led to believe, is to fly in the very face of the divine providence which proffers them.

So thought Giezi, servant of the prophet Eliseus. After his master refused payment for curing the leprosy of the Syrian general Naaman, Giezi ran after him with the story that Eliseus had decided to ask for a contribution for "two young men of the brotherhood" who had just turned up. (Incidentally, concern for others is a characteristic pose of the avaricious. Judas, we recall, bewailed the waste of Mary Magdalene's ointment, alleging it should have been given to the poor. The little old grandmother forever collecting valuables to leave the children, and religious chronically addicted to raising funds for their communities fall into the same category.)

Naaman complied only too happily with Giezi's request, and when the latter returned, the prophet tells him, "So now thou hast received money, and received garments, to buy olive yards, and vineyards, and sheep, and oxen, and menservants, and maidservants." He added, unfortunately, 'But the leprosy of

Naaman shall also stick to thee, and to thy seed forever" (4 Kings 5:26).

The specific malice of avarice certainly doesn't lie in possessing. We can do so legitimately, and possessions in themselves are quite innocent, often serving good purposes. What makes avarice a capital sin is its fundamental, insulting *mistrust of God.* It prompts us to look to things to provide us security, instead of expecting God to satisfy our legitimate needs. We mistrust God, I suppose, because we judge Him by ourselves. In His place we couldn't be capable of such goodness to a creature who had defied us. We simply can't imagine it.

Yet He tells us:

> Therefore I say to you, be not solicitous for your life, what you shall eat; nor for your body, what you shall put on ... Consider the ravens, for they sow not, neither do they reap, neither have they storehouse nor barn, and God feedeth them. How much are you more valuable than they? And which of you, by taking thought, can add to his stature one cubit? If then ye be not able to do so much as the least thing, why are you solicitous for the rest?

> Seek not what you shall eat, or what you shall drink: and be not lifted up on high. For all these things do the nations of the world seek. But your Father knoweth that you have need of these things; But seek ye first the kingdom of God and His justice, and all these things shall be added unto you (Luke 12:22 ff.).

All possession is contrary to hope, because obviously there's no hoping for what we already have, and we tend to rest in it. Preoccupation with the means of survival therefore ends by destroying a theological virtue, one which directly propels us Godward. Avarice, which can't live without the reassurance of the tangible, makes it impossible for us to rise above the material to seek God in spirit and truth.

"Where are you?" is a question God asked not only Adam in the garden; He asks every one of his descendants. Without coming out from behind the trees, we shall never meet God face to face. How do we accomplish this?

The Fathers are ready with their customary three rules conforming in this case to the threefold manifestations of avarice:

1. Relinquish possessions cheerfully and completely according to God's will.

2. Never take back or regret what has once been given.

3. Avoid the superfluous.

These rules are useful, but the Fathers tell us that covetousness can really be conquered only by crushing the head of the serpent. It isn't enough not to possess goods; we must root out the *desire* for them. It's not money, but the love of money which is the root of all evil:

> For it is an impossibility for him who, overcome in the matter of a small possession, has once admitted into his heart a root of evil desire, not to be inflamed presently with the heat of a still greater desire. For the soldier of Christ will be victorious and in safety, and free from all attacks of desire, so long as this most evil spirit does not implant in his heart a seed of this desire ... And so we must not only guard against the possession of money, but also must expel from our souls the desire for it. For we should not so much avoid the results of covetousness, as cut off by the roots all disposition towards it. For it will do no good not to possess money, if there exists in us the desire for getting it.

Avarice is much like lust, which engenders it. Just as many who are not defiled in body can be adulterers in their hearts, so poor people deprived of the goods of this world can in fact be devoured by avarice simply by craving them. All they lack is opportunity, and "the blessing of penury does them no good."

Is it poverty, or greed, which animates so much social unrest today? Blessed are the poor who are poor in spirit. Theirs is the kingdom of heaven.

Finally conquering Hai, the Israelites had learned their lesson: "For booty, Israel took only the cattle and the spoils of the town according to the order Yahweh had given to Joshua. Then Joshua burned Hai, making it a ruin forevermore." With greed no half measures can be taken.

In the forthcoming battle against the Amorrhites, we learn about ...

Anger

After his victory at Hai, Joshua was no longer at leisure to take on his enemies one by one as he chose. Thoroughly aroused to their danger, "when these things were heard of, all the kings beyond the Jordan, that dwelt in the mountains and in the plains, in the places near the sea, and on the coasts of the great sea ... gathered themselves together, to fight against Joshua and Israel with one mind, and one resolution." So it is that when we make some headway against sensuality and possessiveness, our remaining faults combine to overcome us.

As root of all evil, love of money has many allies, unfortunately still at large. As we have seen in the case of Giezi and Ananias and Sapphira among the Amorrhites, "they that dwelt in Gabaon, hearing all that Joshua had done to Jericho and Hai: cunningly devising," decided to resort to trickery (Joshua 9:1-4).

Their ruse was simple. Using elaborate stage dressing, they pretended they had just arrived from a country far away with no local connections, and offered to conclude a treaty of friendship with Joshua. Neglecting to consult God's oracle, Joshua was taken in by the story and "granted them peace and made a treaty with them guaranteeing their lives," furthermore ratifying this by oath. Three days later he found out the truth, but it was too late. He was legally and morally bound.

This teaches important doctrine in reference to anger, showing how it masquerades in order to survive at all costs when threatened. The only way to deal with it once it has betrayed us into tolerating its presence, is the way Joshua took. Although he had to spare Gabaon, he reduced its inhabitants to slavery: "And he gave orders in that day that they should be in the service of all the people, and of the altar of the Lord, hewing wood and carrying water, until this present time, in the place which the Lord hath chosen" (Joshua 9:27).

Like fire, anger is a poor master, but a good servant when kept under control. We must understand that anger is both a passion and a vice. As a passion, it's quite innocent and can be made to serve useful, even religious purposes; for like all passions it's a fuel for internal combustion we can hardly live without, propelling us as it does to fend off evil and at the same time providing the drive necessary to pursue good.

Unfortunately it's always trying to take over. It can mobilize all our sense life, like the five Amorrhite kings who immediately "being assembled together went up ... they and their armies" to recapture Gabaon (Joshua 10:5). Bound to defend his new friends, Joshua soon had a fierce battle on his hands.

Anger has a special affinity to its progenitor, covetousness. Although they are very different in character, both are deceitful, and they operate as partners. Balked of the price of Mary Magdalene's ointment, the covetous Judas fell headlong into deceit and anger when he asked indignantly why it wasn't "sold for three hundred pence, and given to the poor" (John 12:5). Whereas gluttony and lust are connected in that both seek consummation in our flesh, anger and covetousness find rapport in that both find their reason for being excited in something outside us.

When balked of a desire for some external good, anger is normally aroused. Modern psychology is quite correct in postulating that frustration produces anger, but it neglects to add that satisfying desire illicitly produces even deeper anger. This is bound to be so, because in satisfying a sinful craving, we automatically frustrate much higher needs. Or rather, we frustrate our basic need for God who alone can satisfy us. Even when this takes place unconsciously, the damage is still done, and the habitual hostility which results if covetousness isn't checked is all the more deadly for concealing its true origins.

As Joshua asked the Gabaonites, "Why would you impose upon us, saying: We dwell far off from you, whereas you are in the midst of us?" (Joshua 9:22).

Anger deceives on all levels. Just as the covetous man believes himself to be drawn, not by his own diseased volition, but by the attractive goods he finds "far off" outside himself, so it is with anger. Until we progress rather far in self-knowledge, we think we get angry because something "far off" outside ourselves provokes us. "Darn that dripping faucet!" "Now see how you make me lose my temper!" The cause always seems to lie outside us, when actually it's "in the midst of us" like Gabaon.

Adam said it best of all when he told God, "It was the woman you put with me; she gave me the fruit, and I ate it." Here we have a perfect replay of lust producing covetousness and covetousness producing anger. Eve generates desire in Adam for a good outside himself, and when he satisfies it illicitly, he becomes angry—not only with his wife, the fruit and himself, but also with God, whom he dares to blame for putting such enticements before him. The Second Adam was never even tempted to anger by the devil in the desert, because His perfect renunciation of "all the kingdoms of the world" which Satan put before His eyes rendered anger impossible, just as His resistance to gluttony had obviated lust.

The greedy easily become violent, as history proves, but not necessarily. As there are skinny gluttons among us, so there are the calm, cool and furious. Judas, who succumbed totally to love of money, betrayed our Lord with a kiss, first planning how He might be taken "without a disturbance." Like all capital sins, anger varies in form. Need we be surprised that here again, the Fathers discern three?

The Trinitarian image in which we were created determines even our vices:

1. Anger may be the kind called *thumos,* often referred to as "white" anger. It rages and simmers within, but rarely erupts

exteriorly, causing its victim to freeze up rather than boil over. He can be speechless with rage, rooted to the spot. It easily degenerates into resentment. While it lasts the physical effects are painful, all the more so for being bottled up.

2. Or anger may be *orge*. This is the well-known "red" anger, characterized by active indignation. It's easily recognized because it normally erupts into both word and action and is quickly aroused. Although it generally fizzles out sooner than the former, it's capable of almost anything while it rages. It too can be hard on us physically.

3. Finally, anger may be *menis*. Related both clinically and etymologically to mania, it can be very prolonged, in fact informing a whole life-span, perhaps erupting only sporadically into violence. It is characterized by grudge-bearing and deep hostility, well publicized by modern psychiatry.

The Fathers waxed eloquent on the evils which "the deadly poison of anger" brings in its wake:

> For as long as this remains in our hearts, and blinds with its hurtful darkness the eye of the soul, we can neither acquire right judgment and discretion, nor gain the insight which springs from an honest gaze, or ripeness of counsel, nor can we be partakers of life, or retentive of righteousness, or even have the capacity for spiritual and true light ... Nor can we be partakers of wisdom, even though we are considered wise by universal consent, for "anger rests in the bosom of fools."

They tell us that because the wrath of man doesn't accomplish God's justice, anger causes us to lose the control over circumstances that rectitude normally gives us, and we are soon abandoned to our own resources. We end by losing the respect of others, and as long as we are subject to anger we are never free of disturbances and difficulties, even without others bothering us, so penetrating is its disruptive influence. "Be angry, and sin not. Let not the sun go down upon your anger. Give not place to the devil" (Eph. 4:26-27).

St. Paul's injunction brings us back to Joshua. Pursuing the five Amorrhite kings after defeating them at Gabaon, he "spoke to the Lord, in the day that he delivered the Amorrhite in the sight of the children of Israel," and voiced the famous: "Move not, O sun, toward Gabaon, nor thou, O moon, toward the valley of Ajalon!" Whereupon, "the sun and the moon stood still, till the people revenged themselves of their enemies (Joshua 10:12-13).

The Fathers tell us the "sun" here refers not only to the material sun, but especially to the light of reason. When St. Paul warns that it mustn't be allowed to go down on our anger, he wasn't merely forbidding us to bear grudges, taking our anger to bed with us and nursing it through the next day; he was reminding us that if anger gets so out of control that this "sun" of reason eventually goes down in us, we will be left in darkness and helpless prey to the devil, just as Joshua would have fallen before the Amorrhites if God hadn't heard his prayer and prolonged the day.

With reason kept in the ascendant in response to prayer, we can see clearly to battle our spiritual enemies, and proceed to a vigorous mortification of our five senses, much as Joshua's forces were able to pursue all five kings, eventually trapping them in a cave where they were dispatched and buried. There they "put great stones at the mouth thereof, which remain until this day" (Joshua 10:27). Supernaturally sustained reason can rout anger and sensuality totally.

Anger's power to obscure reason is what makes it so dangerous. Literally extinguishing good judgment while we are in its throes, it forces us into wrong decisions, thereby disrupting our active life. It destroys temperance and ends by annihilating prayer life and excluding the Holy Spirit, who will not dwell in a malicious soul. Last but not least, as we shall see, it begets depression, next on the list of deadly sources of sin .

Anger's normal term is murder. In many ways it's the most "social" of all our sins. So often directed against our neighbor, it is capable of dislocating community life at all levels. Its effects are very evident today in the family, in the domestic economy and among nations.

"You have heard that it was said to them of old: Thou shalt not kill. And whosoever shall kill shall be in danger of the judgment. But I say with his brother shall be in danger of the judgment" (Matt. 5:21-22).

Like lust, anger doesn't have to be overtly expressed to be sinful. Whereas the man who looks at a woman lustfully commits adultery with her in his heart, so too, "Whosoever hateth his brother is a murderer" (1 John 3:15). Anger has deep roots, not so much in our hearts, as in our covetousness, which nourishes it. Abbot Joseph, who left us a most beautiful treatise on friendship, says that the first foundation of fraternal charity consists, not in meekness as we might expect, but i5n "contempt for worldly substance and scorn for all things we possess." Love of possessions not only tempts us to put them above brotherly love, but it tempts us to eliminate our brothers if they obstruct our greed. (The close relation between covetousness and abortion should be abundantly clear.)

It's relatively easy to eliminate a show of anger from our words and actions, but this doesn't cure it. Keeping it out of sight can in fact increase it, whereupon it seeks any outlet open to it. As even modern psychiatry can see, suppressed anger can spark any number of psychic and physical ills which seem to bear no relation to their true cause.

Grudge-bearing is a common form of hidden anger. Although it may not directly hurt others, it poisons us interiorly. Hear the Fathers on those who have "let the sun go down" on their anger in this way:

> Prolonging it for several days, and nourishing rancorous feelings against those against whom they have been excited, they say in words that they are not angry, but in fact and deed they show that they are extremely disturbed. For they do not speak to them pleasantly, nor address them with ordinary civility, and they

think that they are not doing wrong in this, because they do not seek to avenge themselves for their upset. But since they either do not dare, or at any rate are not able to show their rage openly and give place to it, they drive in, to their own detriment, the poison of anger, and secretly cherish it in their hearts, and silently feed on it in themselves; without shaking off by an effort of the mind their sulky disposition, but digesting it as the days go by, and somewhat mitigating it after a while.

Unlike lust, anger isn't best cured in solitude, which normally intensifies the faults of those who run away to be freed of the annoyance of others. Lust is truly excited in our bodies at the sight of others we do well to avoid; but the case is different with anger, which doesn't spring from our flesh spontaneously, but from our hearts, like its fellow covetousness. We note the Fathers say "against whom they have been excited," not "who have excited them."

Meekness can't be made to depend on the perfection of others or on their absence from us. This doesn't mean that we must deliberately court the company of those who irritate us, but neither should we avoid them, because our peace is the result of our self-control, not theirs. It's always easier to practice virtue among the virtuous; it's the bad ones who show us up for what we really are.

In solitude the angry man simply takes his anger with him, and even there finds it excited. He may become exasperated with things—machinery that won't start, or a bad pen, the weather, or his dog. It's not enough not to be angry with men, say the Fathers, we mustn't be angry at all. They tell this story:

> A certain brother while he was in the community was restless and frequently moved to wrath. And he said within himself, 'I shall go and live in some place in solitude: and when I have no one to speak to or to hear, I shall be at peace and this passion of anger will be stilled.' So he went forth and lived by himself in a cave.
>
> One day he filled a jug for himself with water and set it on the ground, but it happened that it suddenly overturned. He filled it a second time, and again it overturned: and he filled it a third time and set it down, and it overturned again. And in a rage he caught up the jug and broke it. Then when he had come to himself, he

thought how he had been tricked by the spirit of anger and said, "Behold, here I am alone, and nevertheless he hath conquered me. I shall return to the community, for in all places there is need for struggle and for patience and above all for the help of God."

With their usual intransigence, the Fathers aver there's only one remedy for anger: *Never allow it entry at all, for any cause.*

They don't deny for a minute that, objectively speaking, there is such a thing as just anger. Certainly our Lord exhibited it and did no sin when He thundered against the Pharisees or drove the money-changers from the Temple, but He possessed a perfectly integrated human nature. For practical purposes, subjectively speaking, there's no such thing as just anger. The angry man always thinks his anger is Just, the Fathers note astutely. If he didn't, he wouldn't be angry; and the angrier he gets the more he believes himself justified, because his passion progressively obscures his reason.

St. Francis de Sales, a hot tempered man who became a paragon of gentleness, especially recommended never giving way to anger for any reason. The risk isn't worth it. We must lay down as principle that we have no right to get angry, whatever the provocation. "For the end and aim of patience," say the Fathers, "consists not in being angry with a good reason, but in not being angry." St. Paul advised likewise, "Let all bitterness, and anger, and clamor, and blasphemy, be put away from you, with all malice" (Eph. 4:31).

Being angry with someone who is in fact culpable makes us unfortunately unable to help him remedy his problem. Very often our anger with him even exceeds his offense:

> Or how sayest thou to thy brother: Let me cast the mote out of thy eye; and behold a beam is in thy own eye? ... cast out first the beam out of thy own eye, and then shalt thou see to cast the mote out of thy brother's eye (Matt. 7:4-5).

Nor may we appeal to the so-called anger of God as an excuse for our own. The Fathers scorned such anthropomorphisms which ascribed passion to the deity, teaching clearly that what is termed wrath in God is merely a way of recognizing that "He is the judge and avenger of all the unjust things which are done in this world; and by reason of these terms and their meaning we should dread Him as the terrible rewarder of our deeds, and fear to do anything against His will." He alone may avenge us if we are wronged.

We must keep reminding ourselves, first, that while anger is present in us our reason is on no account to be trusted; second, that we cannot be temples of the Holy Spirit if anger remains in us; and finally, that we,

> ...ought never to pray, nor pour out our prayer to God while we are angry ... Our prayer will lose its effect if our brother has anything against us, just as much as if we were cherishing feelings of bitterness against him in a swelling and wrathful spirit.

Now, that, we might think, is really going a bit far, but we have divine testimony to the same effect:

> If therefore thou offer thy gift at the altar, and there thou remember that thy brother hath anything against thee; Leave there thy offering before the altar, and go first to be reconciled to thy brother: and then coming back thou shalt offer thy gift (Matt. 5:23-24).

Rooting anger out of ourselves doesn't satisfy God's demands; we must run ahead of it as it were and try to remove it even from others. Whether they are angry with us justly or unjustly our Lord disdains to specify. We can't please God—therefore can't be heard in prayer—unless we labor to eradicate any trouble we may have occasioned in another.

Blessed are the peacemakers.

The Abbot Joseph says:

> All things, however useful and necessary they seem, should yet be disregarded that disturbing anger may be avoided, and all things even which we think are unfortunate should be undertaken and endured that the calm of love and peace may be preserved unimpaired, because we should reckon nothing more damaging than anger and vexation, and nothing more advantageous than love.

Not that the good Abbot recommends passivity. He counsels keeping communications open at all costs. Speaking of the dangers of repressing anger without remedying its causes, he cites monks,

> ...who are so hard and obstinate, that when they know that their own feelings are aroused against their brother, or that their brother's are against them, in order to conceal their vexation of mind, which is caused by indignation at the grievance of one or the other, go apart from those whom they ought to smooth down by humbly making up to them and talking with them; and begin to sing some verses of the Psalms. And these while they fancy that they are softening the bitter thoughts which have arisen in their heart, increase by their insolent conduct what they could have got rid of at once if they had been willing to show more care and humility, for a well-timed expression of regret would cure their own feelings and soften their brother's heart ... For by that plan they nourish and cherish the sin of meanness or rather of pride, instead of stamping out all inducement to quarrelling ...
> Sometimes we fancy we are patient because when provoked we scorn to answer, but by sullen silence or scornful motions and gestures so mock at our angry brothers that by our silent looks we provoke them to anger more than angry reproaches would have excited them, meanwhile thinking we are in no way guilty before God, because we have let nothing fall from our lips which could brand us or condemn us in the judgment of men ... Often a feigned patience excites to anger more keenly than words, and a spiteful silence exceeds the most awful insults ...

Anger is aroused not only when we are balked, but also when we feel threatened. The Abbot notes shrewdly that "the nature of the weak is always such that they are quick and ready to offer reproaches and sow seeds of quarrels, while they themselves cannot bear to be touched by the shadow of the very slightest wrongs." Like St. Paul he considers it the duty of the strong to put up with the weak, who often bluster because, besides lack of self-control, they're scared.

A fool immediately showeth his anger: but he that dissembleth injuries is wise" (Prov. 12:16).

Recurring victories over anger should in due course produce magnanimity.

Getting down to procedures the Abbot insists we must "give place unto wrath" as St. Paul put it to the Romans (12:19). This involves channeling it rather than repressing it only to have it explode later. "For the nature of anger is such that when it is given room it languishes and perishes, but if openly exhibited, it bums more and more," the Abbot adds.

He parts company with certain modern schools who counsel getting rid of anger by giving vent to it in some harmless way, maybe by kicking a wastebasket or tearing up an old phone book. True to the tradition of the desert, he maintains we must never willingly give way at all. To give place does not mean to give way.

Giving place means to exercise long-suffering and patience. These are tools of the strong, and they enlarge the heart, "which will have within it safe recesses of counsel, in which the foul smoke of anger will be received and be diffused and forthwith vanish away." Patience immobilizes anger in the heart much as Joshua trapped the Amorrhite kings in the cave, immediately ordering his men to "roll great stones to the mouth of the cave and set careful men to keep them shut up" (Joshua 10:18).

Anger shouldn't be ignored, or left alive long underground, but contained temporarily with a view to prompt liquidation. Ideally, giving place to anger should produce *love*. Fiery old St. Jerome didn't scruple to say, "Love should be full of anger!" Our

Lord had to come and tell us how to achieve something so spectacular:

> You have heard that it hath been said, An eye for an eye, and a tooth for a tooth. But I say to you not to resist evil: but if one strike thee on thy right cheek, turn to him also the other: And if a man will contend with thee in judgment, and take away thy coat, let go thy cloak also unto him.

How beautifully the Lord here teaches the intimate connection between anger and covetousness!

> Give to him that asketh of thee and from him that would borrow of thee turn not away. You have heard that it hath been said, Thou shalt love thy neighbor, and hate thy enemy. But I say to you, Love your enemies: do good to them that hate you: and pray for them that persecute and calumniate you (Matt. 5:38-44).

So it is prayer that does it.

"So Joshua conquered all the country of the hills and of the south and of the plain, and of Asedoth, with their kings ... And all their kings, and their lands he took and wasted at one onset: for the Lord the God of Israel fought for him" (Joshua 10:40, 42).

This completed his subjugation of the "south." From the north enemies more subtle and powerful massed against him, led by the truculent Canaanite,

Depression

At the alert sounded by Jabin, king of Asor, "they all came out with their troops, a people exceeding numerous as the sand that is on the sea shore, their horses also and chariots, a very great multitude" (Joshua 11:4).

The sins dealt with so far require considerable cooperation on the part of the body for their consummation, but after depression is reached they become, as Scripture shows, more "northern." Not primarily residing in our lower faculties and affections, they become progressively more spiritual, more attuned to the workings of the mind and intellect than to the heart and the senses. Depression the first of these, has one foot so to speak still in our physical constitution, but it can arise in us without exterior provocation, sometimes very suddenly.

This might be a good place to stress that the eight capital sins are not capital because they are the most grievous that can be committed. To bear false witness, for instance, can be a deadly violation of a Commandment; yet it doesn't figure on the list of capital sins. What makes these capital is that they are primary *sources* of sin, and as we progress from gluttony to pride, in which they culminate, their capacity for producing more and more sins increases in geometric proportion. (This is precisely why the scholastics placed pride first on their list, for it is capable of spawning everything that preceded it on the Desert Fathers' list.)

As we have seen, anger considered as a passion is no sin at all, but it can produce the sin of anger and offer direct confrontation to charity. Depression is similar. Innocent as the passion of sadness, it is nevertheless capable of degenerating into the deadly sin against hope we call despair.

Of our Lord agonizing in the garden St. Matthew says, "He began to grow sorrowful and to be sad. Then he saith to them: My soul is sorrowful even unto death" (Matt. 26:37-38). Given the Fall, sorrow is part of the human condition, but despair is not. Our Lord permitted himself to suffer sadness in order to lead us to the perfection of hope as revealed in His, "Yet not my will, but thine be done" (Luke 22:42). As He had done no sin in anger, He did none in depression.

That the Fathers speak of depression as sinful comes as a total surprise to our modern way of thinking. What's so reprehensible about giving in to a fit of the blues? Suppose one's temperament just happens to be melancholy? It might be something you ate. The scholastics never included it at all in their list. The Fathers, however, because they were making a subjective survey of sin-as-it-happens, saw quite clearly that depression, like King Jabin of Asor, had the power to activate "a people exceeding numerous as the sand that is on the sea shore" once it got started.

Although it's true, as in alcoholism, that we may have some built-in propensity to depression, the Fathers assure us it's no disease that comes upon us through no fault of our own and over which we have no control. We can be cured with effort on our part without recourse to drugs, special diets, or even human help.

They look at depression squarely for what it is: a dangerous temptation to be resisted by force of will. If we give in to it, we are guilty before God.

A certain brother once asked the Abbot Poemen what he could do to relieve the sadness afflicting him. The old man replied, "Don't look to anyone for anything, condemn no one, disparage no one, and God will give you rest."

This advice may seem *non sequitur* to the uninitiated, but when we remember that depression is preceded on the list of sins by anger, which is sparked in turn by covetousness, the old man's words make good sense.

The three kinds of depression discerned by the Fathers are in fact classified according to their causes:

1. The most common cause of depression is previous anger which has died down. It's common knowledge that transports of rage normally bring on fits of deep depression, as the term "manic-depressive" amply testifies; but even anger momentarily indulged in will issue in sadness more or less prolonged in proportion to the intensity of the anger.

2. Depression naturally results from incurring any loss or disappointment, its gravity depending on the degree of our attachment to our own will. The scholastics, who ignore depression as a source of sin, nevertheless make much of envy, which is certainly closely related to it and which figures on their

list of capital sins. The well-known "pang" of envy is in fact the beginning of depression, an involuntary contraction of the heart at seeing the good of another and desiring it for oneself. Willingly cherished, it produces all the evils of frustration.

3. Finally, depression can result from "unreasonable anxiety of mind."

In this last form the influence of the devil is seldom absent. He can agitate and depress us by natural means when God permits, working on our soul from outside:

> Sometimes without any apparent reason for our being driven to fall into this misfortune, we are by the instigation of our crafty enemy depressed with so great a gloom that we cannot receive with ordinary civility the visits of those who are near and dear to us; and whatever subject of conversation is started by them, we regard it as ill-timed and out of place; and we can give them no civil answer, as the gall of bitterness is in possession of every corner of our heart.

Thus the Fathers shrewdly locate "crabbiness"—not in the context of anger as we might expect—but in the aftermath of depression, where it rightly belongs and thrives with diabolic help and our own negligence in combating it. The devil can further many of his evil objectives by merely inducing or increasing depression, for its effects in any given life are like moth holes in clothing or wormholes in wood, to use the graphic phrases of the Fathers. It doesn't actually destroy the shape of one's life, but it renders it worthless by weakening it to the point of uselessness, just as a moth-eaten garment can't effectively ward off the elements, or worm-eaten wood can't provide proper support.

> It keeps us back at all times from all insight in divine contemplation, and utterly ruins and depresses the mind that has fallen away from its complete state of purity. It does not allow it to say its prayers with its usual gladness of heart, nor permit it to rely on the comfort of reading the sacred writings, nor suffer it to be quiet and gentle with the brethren; it makes it impatient and rough in all the duties of work and devotion: and, as all wholesome

counsel is lost, and steadfastness of heart destroyed, it makes the feelings almost mad and drunk, and crushes and overwhelms them with penal despair.

When willfully given in to, depression has two outstanding effects:

The first regards our neighbor, with whom it makes us totally unable to get along, although we may not directly wish him any harm at all. This is the common plight of the "sorehead," perpetually eaten by bitterness, who can't take a joke and makes a mountain out of every molehill. Everything that happens to him is a major tragedy; no one on earth suffers as he suffers. This can assume the proportions of paranoia, probably the most mysterious complaint to modern psychiatry. Here everyone is out to get him and everyone is suspected of deliberately affronting him. Whatever happens to the severely depressed, he readily believes others are to blame.

As with anger, the Fathers warn those afflicted with depression not to separate themselves from the persons who appear to be causing them annoyance by their conduct, because they are not the real cause of their malady. Like anger, depression springs from within and must be attacked there. Patience,

> ...can keep us at peace even with those who hate peace, so, if it has not been acquired, it makes us perpetually differ from those who are perfect and better than we are: for opportunities for disturbance, on account of which we are eager to get away from those with whom we are connected, will not be wanting so long as we are living among men; and therefore we shall not escape altogether, but only change the causes of dejection on account of which we separated from our former friends.

It's axiomatic that we improve our relations with others when we improve our own character. "We must then do our best to endeavor to amend our faults and correct our manners. And if we succeed in correcting them we shall certainly be at peace, I will not say with men, but *even with beasts and the brute creation.*"

Let would-be controllers of our natural environment take note. Hagiography is replete with stories of the delicate rapport established at times between saints and wild animals, even in this respect following their Lord who, according to St. Mark "was with beasts, and the angels ministered to him" (1:13), after defeating Satan in the desert. Probably the most famous such tale in the Fathers' annals is St. Jerome's, who tells how the great St. Anthony watched two lions dig a grave for his old friend and spiritual father St. Paul the Hermit, who died at one with all creatures in his solitude.

"Much peace have they that love thy law, and to them there is no stumbling-block" (Ps. 118:165). This hardly eliminates suffering, but there is peace, because it is interior. It doesn't depend on the environment, but in fact controls it. Thus becomes clear why the ancient Poemen recommended "not looking to anyone for anything" to the depressed young brother.

The second effect of depression regards ourselves. It is far more serious, for it leads directly to despair of salvation.

First we must note in passing that just as anger can be channeled into fighting our enemies in the Promised Land, so too sorrow can work towards getting rid of them. St. Paul distinguishes two kinds of sadness when he says, "For the sorrow that is according to God worketh penance, steadfast unto salvation; but the sorrow of the world worketh death" (2 Cor. 7:10)..

The good sadness of which he speaks is "obedient, civil, humble, kindly, gentle and patient, as it springs from the love of God, and unweariedly extends itself from desire of perfection to every bodily grief and sorrow of spirit; and somehow or other," note the Fathers, "rejoicing and feeding on hope of its own profit, reserves all the gentleness of courtesy and forbearance, as it has in itself all the fruits of the Holy Spirit."

Worldly dreariness, on the other hand,

...is rough, impatient, hard, full of rancor and useless grief and penal despair, and breaks down the man on whom it has fastened, and hinders him from energy and wholesome sorrow, as it is unreasonable, and not only hampers the efficacy of his prayers, but actually destroys all those fruits of the Spirit.

Far from leading to correction of faults, it leads to personal destruction. This kind must be rooted out completely before it becomes entrenched, and under no circumstances allowed to spread itself God told Joshua before engaging the powerful northern kings in battle to be sure to "hamstring their horses and burn their chariots" (Joshua 11:6), so as to deprive the "people exceeding numerous" of all mobility as soon as possible.

The connection between depression and suicide is a modern truism. "Suicide while despondent" is the usual phrase in journalism. Blues singers, however, have probably described the condition best:

> Feelin' so sad and lonely,
> Runnin' over wid de blues.
> If someone was to give me poison,
> Dat's de kind of death I'd choose!

Depression actually impedes repentance by blocking off hope. The Fathers cite Cain who, falling into depression, couldn't repent of his brother's murder. He could only say, "My iniquity is greater than that I may deserve pardon" (Gen. 4:13). Judas likewise was unable to beg forgiveness. He hanged himself in despair from sterile sorrow at having "betrayed innocent blood." In his case the source of depression is all too easily traced, his covetousness leading to the anger that found its outlet in deicide, this in turn producing the bitterness that actually destroyed him both physically and spiritually .

How can depression be destroyed before it gets its chariots and horses moving?

The Fathers are unanimous in *not* recommending several remedies the world readily prescribes. They don't tell us to bury ourselves in work, for instance, or any other involvement. They don't tell us to run out and make a batch of new and exciting friends, with perhaps a bit of romance thrown in. They don't propose a better sex life, spas, vacations, dietary changes, yoga, elbow-bending or any other exercises. They certainly don't counsel watching the fights to work off the blahs.

As always, they battle the vice in question head on. Because depression is an interior problem, they scorn exterior means. Changing the environment can do no permanent good at all. You'd think, of course, anyone would know that.

Abbot Serapion states flatly that "to overcome depression, anger must first be expelled," thereby effectively hamstringing its horses and burning its chariots. This precaution taken, the Fathers all agree there's really only one remedy: Keeping the mind "constantly occupied with hope of the future and contemplation of the promised blessedness."

In other words, we must deliberately and flagrantly cultivate the theological virtue of hope, even hoping against hope when depression gets really bad. They don't say this is easy, they say it works. Strong faith and serious, steady recourse to prayer and mortification are required. If the Fathers are correct in their diagnosis, obviously the regimen must include avoiding the very remedies the world prescribes.

Need we wonder that the sickness is so common, so resistant to treatment, and spreading all the time? Truly the "plague of modern times," it is assiduously cultured in moral filth. Our society abounds in the gluttony, lust, avarice, and anger it requires for its nourishment.

To appreciate the aptness of the Fathers' remedy, we must remember that the vice of depression belongs entirely to this world; it is bred by this world among people devoted to the things of this world. The cure of depression demands radical conversion, a spiritual process which produces joy as its chief by-product. "All sorrow and dejection must be equally resisted as belonging to this world," say the Fathers; "and being that which works death," must be entirely expelled from our hearts like the spirit of fornication and covetousness and anger. No quarter.

Keeping our minds fixed on our heavenly objectives produces two benefits directly opposed to sadness which automatically make our present, temporal life happier: The accidents of this passing life don't depress us, and we don't get over-elated by prosperity. This eliminates all let-downs. Rather, we learn to "look on each condition as uncertain and likely soon to pass away."

Depression passes with our attachments to the transitory .

Scripture relates that "Asor of old was the head of all these kingdoms," and therefore a most important military objective in Joshua's campaign for control of the north. Certain it is that joy fled and Asor's rule was consolidated when the land of Abraham was over-run by its usurpers. Eventually Joshua, "turning back ... took Asor; and slew the king thereof with the sword" (Joshua 11:10) after he had dealt with the others. Then he burned it to the ground.

By such figures we are told that fullness of joy can never be ours again until all capital sins are brought to bay. Still, we must keep as cheerful as we can, for a depressed spirit is no match for the spiritual foes lying in wait within Asor's sphere of influence. It takes dogged confidence to hold a stable front against the Pherizite, or rather,

Boredom

Acedia, the word the Fathers used to designate the sixth capital sin, defies accurate translation. Literally it means not-caring, but it has overtones of depression, cowardice and sloth which are impossible to convey in one English word.

It's the sin of copping-out, a lazy disgust with everyone and everything, but with the spiritual life in particular. It's well symbolized by the Pherizite, who lived in unwalled villages almost anywhere in the Promised Land, moved around as he pleased, and was therefore hard to locate geographically, much less to corner and isolate. He had no capital city, and neither does boredom. Like the Pherizite, boredom can thrive in any environment, independent of strong central organization or any specific point of reference.

It bears the same close relation to depression that lust bears to gluttony and anger bears to covetousness. Like depression, from which it springs and with which it normally works as teammate, it can arise suddenly without exterior cause. Some of the Fathers identified it with the famous "noonday devil" of the Psalms, "the arrow that flieth in the day" (Ps. 90:6). Caught defenseless in open country, our first impulse under its attack is to run for cover. And that, say the Fathers, is exactly what the noonday devil wants you to do. He will keep you running like a rabbit until you drop in your tracks.

In modern society boredom causes more quiet havoc than the common cold. We get bored to tears. We can be bored stiff, or silly. Because it's a deadly sin, however, we can also literally be bored to death, the spiritual death that overtakes us when finally we run away even from God. Yet, how often does boredom figure in our examinations of conscience? As with depression, we have been led to look on it as simply another of life's afflictions for which we are in no way responsible, and which we are at liberty to dispel by any ready means that offers.

The Fathers ask us to look at it more closely. Their description of its effects on an afflicted monk is full of wry humor and will be recognized by anyone who has ever stifled a yawn:

> When this has taken possession of some unhappy soul, it produces dislike of the place, disgust with the cell, and disdain and contempt of the brethren who dwell with him or at a little distance, as if they were careless or unspiritual. It also makes the man lazy and sluggish about all manner of work which has to be done within the enclosure of his dormitory. It does not suffer him to stay in his cell, or to take any pains about reading, and he often groans because he can do no good while he stays there, and complains and sighs because he can bear no spiritual fruit so long as he is joined

to that society; and he complains that he is ... of no use in the place, as if he were one who, though he could govern others and be useful to a great number of people, yet was edifying none, nor profiting anyone by his teaching and doctrine.

Boredom's hapless victim always finds the other side of the fence greener.

On the other hand, he says that everything around him is rough ... Lastly he fancies that he will never be well while he stays in that place ... unless he leaves and takes himself off from there as quickly as possible. Then the fifth or sixth hour brings him such bodily weariness and longing for food that he seems to himself worn out and wearied as if with a long journey, or some very heavy work, or as if he had put off taking food during a fast of two or three days. Then besides this he looks about anxiously this way and that, and sighs that none of the brethren come to see him.

Eventually:

...he imagines that no cure for so terrible an attack can be found in anything except visiting one of the brethren, or in the solace of sleep alone. Then the disease suggests that he ought to show courteous and friendly hospitalities, and pay visits to the sick, whether near at hand or far off. He talks too about some dutiful religious offices; that those kinfolk ought to be inquired after, and that he ought to go and see them more often; that it would be a real work of piety to go more frequently to visit that religious woman, devoted to the service of God, who is deprived of all support of kindred, etc., etc., and that he ought piously to devote his time to these things instead of staying uselessly in his cell.

Although bred of despairing depression, boredom lacks sufficient drive for outright self-destruction. Working slowly but effectively, it relentlessly goads its prey to *flight*. Where or how matters little, just so he goes, and keeps going. Boredom doesn't seek revenge as anger does, because it actively hates no one.

Seeing no solution to its misery, it seeks only to kill its pain any way it can.

This makes boredom par excellence the sin of the "trip" generation of today, who find momentary alleviation for their anguish by taking a trip of some kind. The young take drugs; the old board tour busses.

Our universe being constructed as it is, there are only two directions in which trips can be taken: we can run in, or we can run out, depending somewhat on our temperament and the opportunities offered. We can take a passive trip and run from boredom by turning inward on ourselves, or we can take an active trip by running to vain involvements with others on the outside. Both are accurately described in the passage on boredom just cited from the Fathers.

The passive trip is essentially some form of *sleep*. This may be no more than natural sleep over-indulged in. Or it may be chronic idling, compulsive eating, television viewing, masturbation, escape literature, pornography, transcendental meditation (the spiritual form of masturbation), or perhaps sauna bathing. Effective as these short-term palliatives may be, it is to drugs that boredom turns for passive trips as by natural compulsion. Their gamut running from dangerous mind-expanders, habit forming "downers" or "uppers" and tranquilizers, to mere tea, coffee and cigarettes, all offer varying degrees of relief from discomfort by the most direct method.

We might be tempted to add alcohol to the list because of its soporific, pain-killing properties when taken in quantity, but such excess is more properly related to over-eating, alcohol being by nature a food. Those who equate drugs with cocktails are on very shaky ground, for whereas drug addiction is an effect of sloth, alcoholism is an effect of gluttony. The remedies cannot be the same in both cases.

The active trip is less easily recognized as a product of boredom. It takes considerable spiritual sophistication to see that both the indolent man who won't move and the man who can't sit still are equally bored, but so they may be. As described in the Fathers' little pen sketch, the latter variety can become obnoxious do-gooders, driving others to exasperation by their "concern" for them. Heaven knows how many travel agencies, political campaigns, health resorts, universities, clubs, charity bazaars and civic projects they keep going. They love discussion groups, conferences, fads, red tape and "meaningful" encounters. Because they tend to be meddlesome and outgoing they naturally seem more numerous than the passive tripper, who is also legion, but quieter and less evident. Most of us take both roles by turn .

Whichever course we take, the noonday devil gains his objective: he has severed us from reality by divorcing us from God's will. Whoever gives in to boredom becomes incapable of discharging his duties of state properly, the *sine qua non* of sanctity. The passive tripper won't do what is required of him; the active tripper does everything but.

From this it's clear that the essential malice of boredom doesn't lie in flight from the disagreeable, or even in flight from self, but in *flight from God.* It is directly opposed to the Third Commandment, which decrees not only that we work six days, but also that we keep the prescribed sabbaths. The passive tripper violates the first part of the ordinance, the active tripper the second, for our acts cannot be ruled by our whims, but by eternal law if we expect to remain in union with God.

As we have already noted, sloth doesn't figure at all on the Fathers' list of capital sins. It is, however, implicit in their notion of *acedia.* Here again, sloth, like boredom, isn't just lying around doing nothing. As a matter of fact doing nothing can be extremely difficult for some temperaments, and strong exertion of will is required to restrain themselves from unnecessary activity. Just as the worst gluttons can often appear abstemious, very lazy people can sometimes look quite energetic, for sloth specifically is *following the line of least resistance* at any given moment. It is a disease of the will.

Sloth and boredom are one in their wholesale, dedicated flight from the Cross. Prayer, which by its very nature becomes tedious as we progress through spells of aridity and abandonment, is effectively cauterized by capitulation to boredom.

> For in truth the soul which is wounded by the shaft of this passion (acedia) sleeps as regards all contemplation of the virtues and insight of the spiritual senses." Again, "For the mind of an idler cannot think of anything but food and the belly, until the society of some man or woman, equally cold and indifferent, is secured, and it loses itself in their affairs and business, and is thus little by little ensnared by dangerous occupations, so that, just as if it were bound up in the coils of a serpent, it can never disentangle itself again and return to the perfection of its former profession.

Because boredom will turn to anything that relieves its pain, it easily finds refuge in all the sins that lie behind it, returning to them as a dog does to his vomit. Obesity, illegitimacy, slander, gambling debts, divorce, abortion, lawsuits and automobile accidents are only some of its grosser by-products. Originally produced by depression, boredom seeks relief in the very gluttony, lust and covetousness which produced the anger which produced the depression which produced the boredom in the first place. Looking over the wealth of filth which this vicious cycle spews around us, we are palpably reminded of Pascal's comment, that all the evils of the world are caused by man's not being able to sit in a room happily by himself.

What to do?
"Stand and fight!" say the Fathers.
John Cassian relates:

> When I was beginning my stay in the desert, and had said to Abbot Moses, the chief of all the saints, that I had been terribly troubled yesterday by an attack of boredom, and that I could only be freed from it by running at once to Abbot Paul, he said, "You haven't freed yourself from it, but rather have given yourself up to it as its slave and subject. For the enemy will henceforth attack you more strongly as a deserter and runaway, since it has seen that you

fled at once when overcome in the conflict: unless on a second occasion when you join battle with it you make up your mind not to dispel its attacks and heats for the moment by deserting your cell, or by the inactivity of sleep, but rather learn to triumph over it by endurance and conflict."

The most reliable nostrum for boredom, we're told, is *work,* preferably silent, and manual. Whether we find it agreeable or not doesn't matter a particle, just so we keep at it.

The Fathers cite St. Paul as their foremost authority. Writing to the Thessalonians, who were apparently troubled with boredom and its baneful consequences in their community, the Apostle tells them to "use your endeavor to be quiet, and that you do your own business, and work with your own hands, as we commanded you" (1 Thess. 4:11).

Explains the Fathers:

> For no one can be restless or anxious about other people's affairs, but one who is not satisfied to apply himself to the work of his own hands ... He cannot possibly walk honestly, even among those who are men of this world, who is not content to cling to the seclusion of his cell and the work of his own hands; but he is sure to be dishonest, while he seeks his needful food; and to take pains to flatter, to follow up news and gossip, to seek for opportunities for chattering and stories by means of which he may gain a footing and obtain an entrance into the houses of others.

> ...He is sure to look with envious eyes on another's gifts and boons, who does not care to secure sufficient for his daily food by the dutiful and peaceful labor of his hands. You see what conditions, and how serious and shameful ones, spring solely from the malady of leisure!

We know only too well today what incalculable evils boredom breeds on our city streets, where "those who will not work are always restless."

"For we have heard there are some among you who walk disorderly, working not at all, but curiously meddling," writes St. Paul to the Thessalonians a second time. "Now we charge them that are such, and beseech them by the Lord Jesus Christ, that, working with silence, they would eat their own bread" (2 Thess. 3:11-12).

Silent manual labor is presented as most beneficial therapy because it provides occupation for the whole person: the body is exercised all the while leaving the mind free to soar to God. Not only does silent labor keep us out of mischief and provide a livelihood, but if we don't need the money ourselves it provides us with a means of extending greater charity to those in need. Regarding Thessalonian trippers, St. Paul minced no words: "This we declared to you: that if any man will not work, neither let him eat" (2 Thess. 3:10).

As for the others, he warned them that boredom is a highly contagious disease, needless exposure to which must be avoided as a matter of course: "And we charge you, brethren, in the name of the Lord Jesus Christ, that you withdraw yourselves from every brother walking disorderly, and not according to the tradition which they have received of us" (2 Thess. 3:6).

The time-hallowed adage of the Egyptian desert has it that, "A monk who works is attacked by only one devil; but an idler is tormented by countless spirits."

Even if we don't need to support ourselves, the Third Commandment alone would bind us to work. At the same time that it orders us to "observe the day of the sabbath, to sanctify it," it also stipulates that "six days shalt thou labor and do all thy works" (Deut. 5:12-13). The second part is as important as the first if we are to become perfect as our heavenly Father is perfect, and imitate His Son, who while on earth told us, "My Father worketh until now, and I work" (John 5:17).

If worse comes to worst, even nonsensical work is better than none. Take the Abbot Paul, for instance, "one of the greatest of the Fathers" according to Cassian. His own inimitable solution to the dilemma of a man on an adequate income in an economic bind is most illuminating:

> While he was living in a vast desert which is called the Porphyrian desert and being relieved from anxiety by the date palms and a small garden, had plenty to support himself and an ample supply of food and could not find any other work to do

which would support him, because his dwelling was separated from towns and inhabited districts by seven days' journey or even more through the desert, and more would be asked for the carriage of the goods than the price of the work would be worth; he collected the leaves of the palms, and regularly exacted of himself his daily task, as if he was to be supported by it.

And when his cave had been filled with a whole year's work, each year he would burn with fire that at which he had so diligently labored: thus proving that without manual labor a monk cannot stop in a place nor rise to the heights of perfection: so that, though the need for food did not require this to be done, yet he performed it simply for the sake of purifying his heart, and strengthening his thoughts, and persisting in his cell, and gaining a victory over acedia and driving it away.

Joshua burned none of the Pherizite towns "that were on hills and high places," but rather appropriated all their spoils after killing the inhabitants (Joshua 11:13-14). Penetrating ever deeper into the Promised Land, he was by now a seasoned veteran, equal to attempting the heights surrounding Jerusalem.

In the highlands to the north of the city lay the strongholds of the Hevite, that treacherous fighter,

Vanity

Preparing to scale the heights of Zion to capture Jerusalem, Joshua met with increasingly cunning last-ditch resistance. "For it was the sentence of the Lord, that their hearts should be hardened, and that they should fight against Israel, and fall, and should not deserve any clemency, and should be destroyed as the Lord had commanded Moses" (Joshua 11:20).

It's a law of the spiritual life that our virtues are best forged in the heat of battle against opposite vices, the more stubborn the vice, the more splendid the consequent virtue. We must believe that God's special favor rests on those who are accorded the most violent opposition to their progress, and it follows that the opposition becomes fiercer as they approach their objective.

The final stage of Joshua's campaign for the Promised Land is therefore fought in the highlands, against vainglory and pride. These two sins stand in a class by themselves in that it is possible to consummate them without the slightest assistance from the body. In them we approximate angelic, luciferian evil.

Asks the Fathers:

> For in what way do those passions need any action of the flesh, which bring ample destruction on the soul they take captive simply by its assent and wish to gain praise and glory from men? Or what act on the part of the body was there in that pride of old in the case of Lucifer, as he only conceived it in his mind and heart? ... And just as he had no one to stir him up to pride, so his thoughts alone were the authors of the sin when complete and of his eternal fall; especially as no exercise of the dominion at which he aimed followed.

Vanity is truly a sin of the heights, because its particular deadliness lies in robbing God himself of the glory which is properly due Him, and appropriating it to ourselves. It is a determined plunge into the unreal, diabolic economy of falsehood and illusion. It is theft from God, from whom we have received not only all we have, but all we are.

"What hast thou that thou hast not received? And if thou hast received," asks St. Paul, "why dost thou glory, as if thou hadst not received it?" (1 Cor. 4:7).

Vanity has other special characteristics. As we have seen, the first six faults are organically connected, one leading into the next so that the complete eradication of one entails wiping out its predecessor. Vainglory and pride, however, are different. They are organically linked to each other as a working pair, as gluttony is to lust, greed to anger, depression to boredom, but they don't spring from their predecessors by overflow as heretofore. They take their occasion from them in a completely different way.

We fall into any one of the six previous faults by allowing ourselves to be overcome by the ones that went before it; but surprisingly enough, we are most likely to fall into vanity just when we have proved ourselves *superior* to some preceding sin. Often a splendid moral triumph provides the most dangerous occasion of all, for vanity and pride flourish all the more vigorously after the other six faults have been eradicated.

Vanity is noted for its ability to infiltrate spiritual areas, for the vain are especially proud of their virtues. There is, in fact, nothing we can't be vain about. This ability to feed on anything and draw material from any quarter makes vanity a most redoubtable guerilla fighter. A master of camouflage, it scorns recognizable uniforms, being content to appropriate any apparel that lies to hand. An adroit opportunist, it deploys extemporaneously through any terrain, as often as not confronting its opponents suddenly with their own captured weapons. Its survival techniques are also highly developed.

John Cassian calls this idle glory "a spirit that takes many shapes, and is changeable and subtle, so that it can with difficulty, I will not say be guarded against, but be seen through and discovered even by the keenest eyes." Although it can be entirely spiritual, it readily makes use of our carnality when this suits its purpose, attacking us on one front or the other, or both at once. Other vices attack us more straightforwardly and in one form at a time, but vanity is equipped to come at us from any direction in true guerilla style.

> For it tries to injure the soldier of Christ in his dress, in his manner, his walk, his voice, his work, his vigils, his fasts, his prayers, when he withdraws, when he reads, in his knowledge, his silence, his obedience, his humility, his patience; and like some most dangerous rock hidden by surging waves, it causes an unforeseen miserable shipwreck to those who are sailing with a fair breeze, while they are not on the lookout for it or guarding against it.

The Fathers used to say this vice attacks on both the left and right, "For where the devil cannot create vainglory in a man by means of his well-fitting and neat dress, he tries to introduce it by means of a dirty, cheap and uncared for style," persuading him, no doubt, to go hippy, to assert his superiority through contempt of accepted values.

> If he cannot drag a man down by honor, he overthrows him by humility. If he cannot make him puffed up by the grace of knowledge and eloquence, he pulls him down by the weight of silence. If a man fasts openly, he is attacked by the spirit of vanity. If he conceals it for the sake of despising the glory of it, he is assailed by the same sin of pride.

In other words, even in the very act of overcoming temptation to vanity, we become vain of our virtue. Alas, admitted the Fathers, vanity is like an onion. The more you strip its layers, the more you uncover. Even solitude is no protection. Run from it as we will, it only infects whatever we run to. Other vices grow weak as we fight them, but vanity only grows stronger. It's the sin of the goody-goody, the grandstand artist, the apple polisher, seeking approval of others to the point of disregarding the judgment of God, who alone sees truly and rewards.

Our Lord warned His followers:

> Take heed that you do not your justice before men, to be seen by them: otherwise you shall not have a reward of your Father who is in heaven. Therefore when thou dost an almsdeed, sound not a trumpet before thee, as the hypocrites do in the synagogues and in the streets, that they may be honored by men.

Unfortunately, even running from our audience won't preserve us from vanity, because there's always one spectator who insists on attending our every performance: ourselves. Until we can ignore this ubiquitous fan, we have little hope of controlling the vice. "When thou dost alms, let not thy left hand know what thy right hand doth," counsels our Lord, so delicate is the situation (Matt. 6:1-3).

The Fathers have an amusing anecdote to contribute to the subject. John Cassian recalls:

> I remember an elder, when I was staying in the desert of Skete, who went to the cell of a certain brother to pay him a visit, and when he had reached the door heard him muttering inside, and stood still for a little while, wanting to know what it was that he was reading from the Bible or repeating by heart (as is customary) while he was at work. And when this most excellent eavesdropper diligently applied his ear and listened with some curiosity, he found that the man was induced by an attack of this spirit to fancy that he was delivering a stirring sermon to the people.
>
> And when the elder, as he stood still, heard him finish his discourse and return again to his office, and give out the dismissal of the catechumens, as the deacon does, then at last he knocked at the door, and the man came out and met the elder with the customary reverence, and brought him in and (for his knowledge of what had been his thoughts made him uneasy) asked him when he had arrived, for fear lest he might have taken some harm from standing too long at the door: and the old man joking pleasantly replied, "I only got here while you were giving out the dismissal of the catechumens."

Because vanity is so inextricably mixed in with the genuine virtues we are bound to cultivate, whoever tries to uproot it finds himself like the farmer in the Gospel who finds his good wheat field sown with weeds. At first he can do only as our Lord suggested in the parable and "let them both grow till the harvest," because to do otherwise at the outset would destroy too much of the good crop.

In the latter stages of the campaign against the eight vices we come to recognize and accept the fact that God will not make saints of us overnight, nor will He destroy our enemies without long and strenuous cooperation on our part. We are taught patience and humility by learning to bear with the evil we see ever more clearly in ourselves, and which for the moment we are powerless to eradicate. We are furthermore taught that *evil has its uses*. Despite His own hatred of it, God permits it to continue for His glory and our greater good.

Just before the Israelites entered the Promised Land to attack their enemies, God had told them through Moses, "I will not cast them out from thy face in one year: lest the land be brought into a wilderness, and the beasts multiply against thee. By little and little I will drive them out before thee, till thou be increased, and dost possess the land" (Exodus 23:29-30).

Vanity has its uses. Human respect keeps many "wild beasts" under control who would otherwise finish off raw recruits long before they reached Jerusalem. It's possible, after all, to live a good ethical life through motives of vanity alone where true love of God is lacking, as the Pharisees were doing. For instance, how many of us are simply too vain to get drunk, or beat our wives, or lose our tempers in public? How many of us control gluttony mercilessly merely through horror of becoming fat and unsightly? Or give liberally to charitable causes for income tax purposes, or fear of peer disapproval as tightwads?

Abbot Serapion plainly considered vanity a better deterrent than none at all, especially against carnal sins. He found it fortunate that "those troubled by the spirit of fornication," for instance, should form:

> ...an idea of the dignity of the priesthood or of reputation among men, by which they may be thought saints and immaculate: and so with these considerations they repel the unclean suggestions of lust, as deeming them base and at least unworthy of their rank and reputation; and so by means of a smaller evil they overcome a greater one. For it is better for a man to be troubled by the sin of vainglory, than for him to fall into the desire for fornication, from which he either cannot recover at all or only with great he has fallen.

The fast disappearing social stigma once attached to sexual deviations is much to be deplored in modern cultures which boast no other curbs. The power of vanity can hardly be underestimated. It can make a man "utterly indefatigable" says the Abbot. His confrere Abbot Macarius provided a very neat explanation to a brother who asked him why he was troubled with hunger as early as the third hour in the desert, whereas in the monastery he had often scorned food for a whole week without feeling hungry. "Because," replied he, "here there is nobody to see you fast, and feed and support you with his praise of you; but there you grew fat on the notice of others and the food of vainglory."

Although there is less harm in yielding to vanity in such circumstances than yielding to fornication, unfortunately it is more difficult to extricate ourselves from vanity's stranglehold once it establishes itself as motive principle. Like greed, vanity only increases with age, gorging on the achievements of a lifetime. Useful in a limited way to beginners, vanity proves fatal in the last stages, destroying the very foundations of faith and severing us from God.

At the Sheep Pool our Lord told the Pharisees, "I receive not glory from men. But I know you, that you have not the love of God in you ... How can you believe who receive glory one from another: and the glory which is from God alone, you do not seek?" (John 5:41-44).

The closed circuit mutual admiration society can be found or established anywhere. It provides mighty support for its members in this life, even against God himself. Naturally allied to ambition, vanity can drive even cowards to assume heavy responsibility if necessary. "Fly from women and bishops!" ran the ancient maxim of the desert. Both made deadly appeals to a poor monk's vanity, the first by luring him into the things of this world, the latter by instilling in him vain desires for the spiritual ascendancy conferred by Ordination.

Vanity can't be eliminated by strong-arm tactics, say the Fathers; it's too clever, too much a part of us to be seen clearly. This being the case, *prevention* is far more important than when dealing with the other sins.

Unless young people are actually told about it, they can't be expected even to recognize it. This is especially true in a society like our own which deliberately cultivates it to a high degree, leading youth to believe that the judgment of the peer group is the norm of right action. With the plethora of honor societies, constant appeals to competitiveness, useless exhibitions of talents and skills before any audience that will gather, it's small wonder that vanity flourishes, positively encouraged as a virtue. No more powerful motivation can be found to bend youth to any collective will.

At the same time, total immersion in mass media feeds all of us a constant diet of illusion, administered surreptitiously through our senses by ever-improving subliminal techniques. These are the very methods employed by the devil in his own brainwashing programs, and anyone who gives in to them soon loses his ability to distinguish reality. Adolf Hitler put it in a nutshell with his famous dictum that a lie told often enough and loud enough is accepted as truth.

With a view to healthy prevention, the Fathers describe three forms of vanity we must watch for in ourselves:

1. As beginners, we usually take empty satisfaction in anything good we *have,* or happen to *be,* whether or not this involves boasting of it or congratulating ourselves on it. Occasions can range all the way from good looks, brains, wealth or family connections to a good singing voice or sex appeal, perhaps the ability to wiggle our ears. It might even be good health. It's possible to be vain of never catching colds or poison ivy.

2. The second degree of vanity concerns not what we have in possession, but what we *could have,* or *could be.* Inasmuch as the vice of vanity resides largely in the imagination, we find it equally easy to entertain convictions of the worldly success which would be ours if we weren't too virtuous, or too circumscribed, to stoop to the necessary means of attaining it. This permits us to be vain of an untold number of accomplishments we'll never have to labor for, like the lady in *Pride and Prejudice* who would have been very proficient at the harpsichord "had she ever studied."

As we progress spiritually, we are tempted to muse on the great things we've given up in order to do God's will more perfectly, what we could have been if we weren't so dedicated to duty. Religious ponder what they could have become in the world; housewives are certain that if marriage hadn't interfered with their careers, thousands would be at their feet; husbands and fathers feel held back by the hostages they have given to fortune, etc.

3. In advanced stages, vanity can exist exclusively in desires, pipe dreams made out of whole cloth, in which we always play the leading role. Gradually severing all ties with reality "as if deluded by a profound slumber," say the Fathers, the victim "is often led away by the pleasure of such thoughts and filled with such imaginations that it cannot even look at things present, or the brethren, while it enjoys dwelling upon these things, of which with its wandering thoughts it has waking dreams, as if they were true."

Because it is a vice which can have no existence in fact, vainglory can culminate only in the unreal, even in delusion and madness. The very word vanity means *emptiness*. Inasmuch as everything we have or are is not ours, but God's, to assign anything to ourselves automatically removes us from reality and establishes us in illusion. Our Lord told the Pharisees, "If I were to seek my own glory, that would be no glory at all; my glory is conferred by the Father" (John 8:54). Even the Son of God would claim nothing!

Not being so foolhardy as to fight vanity head on, we may nevertheless follow three rules of conduct in an effort to sidestep it:

1. First, we must be careful never to do anything for the sake of applause from others.

2. Then, work once begun must be guarded from vainglory as we go along. Many a good work begun in the spirit ends in the flesh for want of constantly renewing and purifying our initial intention.

3. Finally, we must make it a habit to avoid anything unnecessary, at all times, especially anything that would bring notice on ourselves .

If we can't hold this line, we can hardly expect to dislodge the long-entrenched Jebusite who holds Jerusalem. Looking down on us from the citadel as we painfully begin to scale the upper slopes of Mt. Zion, he prepares to grant us no quarter, blocking every access. He is ...

Pride

Joshua's men have now reached "the sin of the perfect." The devil himself couldn't commit a bigger one.

Although last in the order of combat against sin-as-it happens in execution, pride is first in origin and intention, because from the beginning all these others were committed in view of it. They all pre-supposed it in much the same way Joshua had Jerusalem in view when he attacked Jericho, Hai, Asor and all the other cities that stood in his way. This the scholastics well saw when they placed it at the head of their list of capital vices.

Every sin is a sin of pride in that it carries out a desire for one's own will as opposed to the Creator's intention and our own true God-given nature. In practice, it marks the pinnacle of gluttony, raised to spiritual status, and it persists long after lesser gluttonies have been eradicated. Like the devil who first infected us with his sin, pride's ultimate object is to swallow God himself, going the final step beyond vanity, which merely seeks to absorb His glory and attributes. The scholastics didn't list vanity at all among the capital sins, being content to consider it as a form of pride; the Fathers, however, always at pains to emphasize practical differences, make a sharp distinction between wanting to appropriate what God *has* and wanting to appropriate what God *is*.

They define pride as "an evil beast that is most savage and more dreadful than all the former ones, chiefly trying those who are perfect, and devouring with its dreadful bite those who have achieved the consummation of virtue." It is the super-sin of the Pharisee in the parable who prays, "O God, I give thee thanks that I am not as the rest of men, extortioners, unjust, adulterers, as also is this publican. I fast twice in a week: I give tithes of all that I possess" (Luke 18:11-12).

Seeking to place itself above others to the point of equality with God, the fullness of pride can't be reached until all lesser vices have been subjugated. These last attack a specific virtue. Gluttony, for instance, destroys temperance; lust, purity; anger, patience, etc.; but pride destroys all virtues at one fell swoop by falling on them like the Jebusite from the heights.

The richer we are in virtue, the prouder we can become. Pride is par excellence the evil spirit who returns to the soul of the man practiced in virtue, "finding it empty, swept and tarnished" and "then he goeth, and taketh with him seven other spirits more wicked than himself, and they enter in and dwell there: and the last state of that man is made worse than the first" (Matt. 12:44-45). Pride takes pride in attacking the best. It turned Lucifer from a seraph to a devil.

"His portion is made fat, and his meat dainty" (Hab. 1:16) .

The Fathers distinguish two kinds of pride, carnal and spiritual. Relatively few people are tempted to the latter, because few seek perfection that seriously. For those who do, carnal pride is disposed of earlier in the campaign.

As a matter of fact it's interesting to note that Adonisedec, the Jebusite king of Jerusalem, had in fact led the coalition against Joshua after the destruction of Hai and was one of the five kings who was exterminated in the cave. As representative of carnal pride, he disappears with ruthless mortification of the five senses, on whom he depends for support. The vast majority of Christians never get beyond this stage, and the Fathers ruefully admit that the devil need rarely tempt us with more than carnal pride, inasmuch as we continue entangled in earthy passions.

Nor are the symptoms of carnal pride hard to detect, they tell us. These are disobedience, lack of gentleness towards others, refusal to remain on the same level as others, a resistance to giving up possessions, bragging, and a marked preference for being self-supporting. They also mention wanting to live a long life. How refreshing! The current hypochondria and preoccupation with physical well-being, miracle drugs and transplants bespeaks all too eloquently the basic disorder galloping untreated through our materialistic society.

Among the faults eventually produced by carnal pride is materialism, joined to inability to take instruction from others and an outright distaste for spiritual subjects. The proud take all criticism personally, are prone to alternating between extremes of boisterous merriment (joy! joy!) and glum silence (doom! doom!), their passions being little disciplined, and they easily hold grudges. Apologies from others especially infuriate them, note the Fathers, because they feel they must excel even in humility!

The catalogue continues with various unmistakable outward signs of their problem: a loud voice, swaggering-gait, bitter silence, noisy laughter, excessive talking, impudence in insulting others coupled with a thin-skinned inability to receive in kind. They can't give good advice, but are zealous in voicing their opinions. Ever intent on their own objectives, they find it hard to give way to others.

For these ills caused by carnal pride the Fathers offer the usual triple medication, three nostrums which won't eliminate the disease entirely, but will at least relieve the painful symptoms:

1. Make it a practice always to *place ourselves below others,* both mentally and actually. Even the necessary exercise of authority is no obstacle to this, if we remember that authority is essentially a service to those we must govern.

2. *Bear all affronts with patience,* meditating the while on our Lord's Passion and all He endured even though He was the Son of God and supremely innocent.

3. Keep in mind at all times the *shortness of this life,* which renders the solicitations of pride hardly worth the trouble .

So much for carnal pride. Spiritual pride is something else again.

Although it's true Joshua had executed King Adonisedec of Jerusalem at the close of the southern campaign, this had been possible only because the luckless monarch had allied himself with Joshua's lesser foes, and was cornered far from his stronghold on Zion. We can in fact eliminate pride as long as it is merely part of some lesser vice. Specifically, this is what "carnal" pride is, wedded to the body and its appurtenances.

Pride in pure form, proper and diabolic, as represented by the Jebusite nation itself, was never completely conquered by the Israelites on its own territory or driven out of Jerusalem at all. The tribe of Benjamin, to whom Joshua eventually allotted the city, had to be content to live alongside these people as best it could. Even in the days of Solomon, Areuna the Jebusite is recorded as still owning the threshing-floor on which the Temple was built.

The conclusion is clear. Painful as it is, we must learn to live with it.

Like our primal gluttony, it is a sorry fact of life, a consequence of the fall calculated to humiliate us. Admitting this is already the beginning of humility.

Scripture warns us God resists the proud, because pride takes God himself for its adversary, unlike other sins, which spend themselves against men. God had to abase himself to earth, becoming human like ourselves, to show us what true humility is.

Pride says, "I will ascend into heaven, I will exalt my throne above the stars of God, I will sit in the mountain of the covenant, in the sides of the north. I will ascend above the height of the clouds, I will be like the most High" (Is. 14:13-14).

To which the God-Man answers, "Learn of me, because I am meek, and humble of heart" (Matt. 11:29).

Speaking through Pharaoh, pride says, "I know not the Lord!" (Ex. 5:2).

And Christ answers, "And if I shall say that I know him not, I shall be like to you, a liar" (John 8:55).

"The river is mine, and I made myself!" boasts pride (Ez. 29:3).

"I cannot of myself do any thing," our Lord humbly admits (John 5:30).

We are hereby divinely taught that *the only remedy for pride lies in referring all things absolutely to God,* and in *never relying on our own strength alone.* Like the good thief on Calvary, we must acknowledge that we aren't saved by our own works, but by God's mercy.

There is an insistent refrain throughout the story of Joshua whereby God periodically reminds the fighting Israelites, "I brought you into the land beyond the Jordan; they made war on you and I gave them into your hands; you took possession of their country because I destroyed them before you." As long as they obeyed His commands, God repeatedly turned the tide of battle in their favor, if necessary sending hornets and hailstones against their adversaries, or even causing the sun to stand still.

Without God we can do nothing. We can't even desire perfection without His special inspiration. Nevertheless our human cooperation is essential, for without it God will not help us. Zealous to correct an Augustinianism pushed too far in his own day, John Cassian exhibits a quasi-Pelagianism in his insistence on strenuous human effort, but this effort is minimized at our peril, for God helps those who help themselves.

Even knowing this is God's gift.

A person grown cold in pride normally takes one of two courses: He will either retire into some kind of lofty seclusion, convinced that other people can't possibly understand him and are merely impeding his growth in perfection; or he will attempt to organize a special closed society where he can gather together a choice, enlightened few whom he can instruct and dominate.

Both varieties are so plentiful in the modern world, where everyone is doing his thing either alone or in groups, there is little need to point them out. Nor is there much need to dwell on the inescapable consequences, quite accurately predicted by the canny old Fathers.

These remark with customary candor that spiritual pride is no guarantee against carnality. Quite the contrary. Although we might expect the spiritually proud to despise sensuality as unworthy of them—as indeed they often do—in practice they often fall into its lowest aberrations. It is observable fact that the higher they rise in pride, the lower they fall into the lesser sins.

"Every proud man is an abomination to the Lord," says Proverbs, "though hand should be joined to hand, he is not innocent" (16:5). And the punishment fits the crime, for impurity of soul leads by a secret but direct path to carnal impurity, the infection of the flesh being merely the carnal expression of the underlying spiritual uncleanness. Sexual laxity is the most psychosomatic of diseases; heresiarchs throughout history have exhibited a congenital susceptibility to it.

John Cassian relates:

> I knew one of the brethren who confessed to a most admirable elder that he was attacked by a terrible sin of the flesh: for he was inflamed with an intolerable lust, with the unnatural desire of suffering rather than of committing a shameful act. Then the other like a true physician at once saw through the inward cause and origin of this evil, and sighing deeply, said, "Never would the Lord have suffered you to be given over to so foul a spirit unless you had blasphemed against Him."
>
> And he, when this was discovered, at once fell at his feet on the ground, and struck with the utmost astonishment, as if he saw the secrets of his heart laid bare by God, confessed that he had blasphemed with evil thoughts against the Son of God. Whence it is clear that one who is possessed by the spirit of pride, or who has been guilty of blasphemy against God—as one who offers a wrong to Him from whom the gift of purity must be looked for—is deprived of his uprightness and perfection and does not deserve the sanctifying grace of chastity.

Probing blasphemy as a source of unnatural vice might yield interesting results today. As we have already seen, the inner connection between pride and sexual deviations was repeatedly stressed by the Fathers:

> He who is puffed up with swelling pride of heart is given over to most shameful confusion to be deluded by it, that when thus humbled, he may know that he is unclean through impurity of the flesh and knowledge of impure desires—a thing which he had refused to recognize in the pride of his heart; and also that the shameful infection of the flesh may disclose the hidden impurity of the heart, which he contracted through the sin of pride, and that through the patent pollution of his body he may be proved to be impure, who did not formerly see that he had become unclean through the pride of his spirit.

That today we accept sexual impurity as merely natural reveals how hardened in pride we have become. We live in delusion.

Hard won humility, as saints know, is nothing but coming to grips with reality. Finally divesting ourselves of illusion, we admit we have fallen from what God made us to be, and we continue in existence only because He sustains us. Take it or leave it. This is why the perfection of humility can never be ours without the practice of the evangelical counsels. Only through poverty, chastity and obedience can we relinquish everything to God in filial love, thereby divesting ourselves of a world of vanity.

Pride being a delusion that our excellence is autonomous, it is constantly declaring its independence of God, aspiring to a self-subsistence which is God's alone. Today it declares that our modern world, now evolved to maturity through technological progress, is finally free to manipulate the universe and the laws of nature as its own intelligence directs. Not content with usurping God's gifts, as mere vanity does, it wants to usurp what God is, to *become* God.

By presuming to satisfy them at will, it claims freedom from all the "gluttonies" which in their backhanded way proclaimed our dependence on Him. Unfortunately, by diverting them to itself as center, pride enslaves us to every one of them. It sends us straight back to Egypt, the quintessence of the welfare state where all physical wants are satisfied at the price of human liberty.

In no time at all, we are faced with riots and insurrections on the part of all the enemies we had only just begun to control. The Egyptians catch up with us, and suddenly Amorrhites, Gergezites, Hevites, Pherizites and many other sons of Ham whose existence we had hardly suspected until now, have arisen out of nowhere and are swarming all over us. The Promised Land must be won all over again!

Be of good cheer. God Knows .

Scripture closes its account of Joshua's campaigns with the laconic, "And the land rested from wars" (Joshua 11:23). For a time, that is.

It's true the Promised Land was officially apportioned out by lot among the twelve tribes, but their tenure was precarious. As in the spiritual life, not only did many large sectors remain unpenetrated, but some which had been subdued revolted and eventually regained control. It's a fight to the finish, where no co-existence is possible.

"Each fault has its own special corner in the heart," say the Fathers, "which it claims for itself in the recesses of the soul, and drives out Israel, i.e., the contemplation of holy and heavenly things, and never ceases to oppose them. For virtues cannot possibly live side by side with faults." St. Paul asks, "What fellowship hath light with darkness? And what concord hath Christ with Belial? Or what part hath the faithful with the unbeliever?" (2 Cor. 6:14-15).

> But as soon as these faults have been overcome by the people of Israel ... then at once the place in our hearts which the spirit of concupiscence and fornication had occupied will be filled by chastity. That which wrath had held will be claimed by patience.

That which had been occupied by a sorrow that works death will be taken by a godly sorrow and one full of joy. That which had been wasted by acedia will at once be tilled by courage. That which pride had trodden down will be ennobled by humility.

The apportionment of land among the tribes was in fact little more than an assignment of territory which it was their responsibility to conquer and keep under subjection. The mighty Joshua, one of the most powerful figures of Christ in Scripture, had done the hard work, but it remained for following generations to consolidate his conquest.

We aren't privileged to progress in an orderly march from victory to victory as Joshua and Christ did, beginning with gluttony in Egypt and ending with pride in Jerusalem. The baptized Christian begins in the Promised Land, already surrounded at birth by a multitude of different enemies hoping to exterminate him.

Abbot Serapion informs us:

> You must know that our battles are not all fought in the same order. As the attacks are not always made on us in the same way, each one of us ought also to begin the battle with due regard to the character of the attack which is especially made on him in particular, so that one man will have to fight his first battle against the fault which stands third on the list, another against that which is fourth or fifth. And in proportion as faults hold sway over us and the character of their attack may demand, so we too ought to regulate the order of our conflict in such a way that the happy result of a victory and triumph succeeding may assure our attainment of purity of heart and complete perfection.

In other words, we begin to fight wherever we are, God help us.

In his last exhortation to the people before he died, Joshua once more stressed the fact that "the Lord your God ... himself hath fought for you." Never must we make the mistake of thinking we can overcome our enemies by our efforts alone, indispensable as these may be. "The Lord your God will destroy them, and take them away from before your face" (Joshua 23:3,5). The refrain never varies.

Recapitulating the master strategy to which all lesser tactical and logistical objectives must conform, he warns us:

> Take courage, and be careful to observe all things that are written in the book of the law of Moses: and turn not aside from them neither to the right hand nor to the left: lest after that you are come in among the Gentiles, who will remain among you, you should swear by the name of their gods, and serve them, and adore them (Joshua 23:6-7).

In this admonishment lies the whole of ascetical theology.
As long as the Israelites were faithful:

> ...one of you shall chase a thousand men of the enemies: because the Lord your God himself will fight for you, as he hath promised ... But if you will embrace the errors of these nations that dwell among you, and make marriages with them, and join friendships, know ye for a certainty that the Lord your God will not destroy them before your face, but they shall be a pit and a snare in your way, and a stumbling-block at your side, and stakes in your eyes, till he take you away and destroy you from off this excellent land, which he hath given you" (Joshua 23:10-13).

Later the Book of Judges tells us that, "After the death of Joshua the children of Israel consulted the Lord, saying: Who shall go up before us against the Canaanite, and shall be the leader of the war?" (1:1).

There wasn't a moment to lose, nor is there today, for the battle continues as fiercely as ever.

Postscript

Devil-fighting isn't generally thought of as the first consequence of devotion to the Mother of God. If we progress in intimacy with her, however, we soon realize something of what almighty God meant when he said to Satan in Eden, "I will make you enemies of each other: you and the woman, your offspring and her offspring."

Suddenly, her enemies are our enemies. By the time we wake up to the situation, we're already in the thick of battle, locked in mortal combat with an invisible foe who seems to specialize in fouls. Devil-fighting, we learn, is basic Christian warfare. St. Paul nevertheless warned us at the outset that we aren't pitted against human enemies in this life, but against the "princedoms and powers, against those who have mastery of the world in these dark days, against malign influences in an order higher than ours" (Eph. 6, 12).

Very early young mother Church developed practical doctrine for her children on this important subject, so they wouldn't be defenseless against diabolic logistics and would know what to expect. Much of the pioneering was done by those ancient stalwarts we call the Desert Fathers. Following the example of the Lord himself, they purposely stationed themselves in the wilderness to challenge the devils to hand to hand combat on their own ground.

One of these was the monk Serenus, noted for his outstanding chastity and purity of heart, which rendered him invincible against the powers of darkness. Speaking from his own experience and that of many saints before him—the great St. Anthony was one—he left us two priceless conferences which lay the workings of devils before us in considerable detail.

It would be foolhardy for a servant of the Immaculata not to listen to what he has to say. No figment of the imagination, nor mere abstract "personification of evil" as some like to think, the devil is a real person, possessing intelligence and will, and he hates us inexorably.

Abba Serenus begins this discourse by making us aware of the terrible inconstancy of our thoughts, a condition resulting from original sin. He stresses the direct relation between our wavering minds and our susceptibility to the devil's wiles in our mentally and morally weakened state. The devil knows that if he is to make us sin he must first get us to think about it, to entertain the thought of it interiorly.

"Why do you have such wicked thoughts in your hearts?" our Lord asked the Pharisees (Matt. 9:4). Sin is never committed from the outside in, although it might look that way; it's committed from the inside out. No temptation could gain entry into a properly God-oriented, disciplined mind. Inasmuch as "no one can be deceived by the devil but one who has chosen to yield to him the consent of his own will ... it is therefore clear," says Abba Serenus, "that each man goes wrong from this: that when evil thoughts assault him he does not immediately meet them with refusal and contradiction." If you crush the head of the serpent before he can strike, you don't have to worry about the rest of him.

Having made this clear, Abba Serenus then proceeds to acquaint us with certain basic facts. First he bucks us up by telling us what we don't have to worry about:

For instance, *there can be no actual union between a human soul and the devil,* although both are spirits. This is possible only with God. Even in cases of possession, the devils can govern only the body, "laying on them an enormous intolerable weight which overwhelms the soul with foulest darkness and interferes with its intellectual powers." In the case of Job, we learn that God has to give permission for even this power over the body. The soul always remains free, no matter what antics the devil may put the body through.

Equally consoling is the fact that *unclean spirits cannot read our thoughts,* any more than good angels can. Both, however, are able to influence our thoughts by way of the imagination, which makes use of sensible images. Devils can excite feelings in us, such as lust, anger or despair. They can also deduce what we must be thinking by watching us closely and noting the effects they're producing in us. Even clever human beings can do this.

This is one good reason why exterior deportment is always important, even when we're alone. Devils study us like thieves planning to rob a bank. Wanting to bring down a particular soul, they find his weaknesses by throwing out various evil suggestions and observing which ones get favorable responses. They get to know us better than we know ourselves.

Not every devil has the power to suggest every passion. They have their specialties, and in order to implant their particular vice, they have to await the opportune time and place. This is why the Church has always taught us to avoid occasions of sin as we would sin itself.

Devils attack us systematically, taking their turns in order by prearranged plan according to opportunity. We know there's neither true concord nor brotherly agreement in hell, but common interest, sheer necessity, or hope of success can organize them temporarily for a kill. This is inevitable, because they can attack us only through our fixed inclinations at particular times. They can't, for instance, tempt us to silly giggling and anger at the same time. Our very nature forces them to use system in their temptations.

Devils vary in strength, boldness and malice. When one is defeated, a stronger one takes over. As we progress in virtue our struggles get fiercer, because Christ is the referee and matches opponents justly. We have his word for it that we'll not be tried beyond our strength.

Devils don't battle without effort on their part. It's a real fight, with exertion and exhaustion on both sides. They experience pain, anxiety and depression when they're pitted against saints and strong souls who put up serious resistance. They know grief and confusion at losing, and a certain malicious delight in winning. "Stand your ground!" says St. Paul (Eph. 6:14). We actually gratify hell when we lose.

Still, *their power to hurt us doesn't depend on the devils themselves.* This occurs only when permitted by God, in the measure He decrees to test us, or as punishment for our sins or negligence. Without His express permission, they couldn't even enter the Gerasene swine.

Their power over us nevertheless increases or decreases according to the effectiveness of the resistance they meet with. The less opposition we give them, the greater control they gain over us. In preparing a victim for bodily possession, they move through three stages, says Abba Serenus: First they take possession of his mind and thoughts; then they rob him of his fear of God; and finally they destroy all possibility of recollection and meditation on spiritual things. At this point they take over because they have in fact won his consent.

Here Abba Serenus has a message all too pertinent to our modern scene. He says that *men possessed by sin are more wretched than those possessed bodily by the devil,* because they are the devil's slaves without knowing it. This gives Satan a much freer hand and leisure to operate without arousing suspicion. This constitutes the worst punishment God can deal out in this life, because the unrepentant sinner not punished on earth is reserved for hellfire. Saints, on the other hand, are proverbially sent much suffering and trouble, the devil being allowed power against them for their greater glory and purification.

There's rarely a dull moment. *Unclean spirits have many different desires and wishes,* just as we do, says the Abba, because like us they have wills and personalities. Some, like poltergeists, are relatively harmless, but annoying. They seem to be intent on tiring us out rather than actually hurting us, by playing bad practical jokes, breaking car axles or perpetrating other minor sabotage, and they seem to infest certain localities by preference. Others, on the other hand, are extremely ferocious, like the ones our Lord encountered near the tombs in Gerasa, whom no one dared approach or restrain. These delight in bloodshed and do all they can to foment war and violence.

Still others specialize in exciting lust and promoting impurity. Some are seized with empty pride and excel in delusions of all kinds. Others are expert liars, inspiring men to blasphemy and heresy. One of these openly boasted to the Fathers that he was the originator of the Arian heresy professed through the mouths of Arius and Eunomius. St. Paul in fact writes to St. Timothy of certain Christians who were "giving heed to seducing spirits and doctrines of devils speaking lies in hypocrisy" (1 Tim. 4:1-2). Heretical devils are extraordinarily intelligent and delight in deluding victims with high I.Q.'s who aren't also humble and obedient.

Such are our enemies, and God's and his blessed Mother's. They are legion. Be sober, be watchful.

St. Michael, the Archangel, defend us in battle!

Revisiting Sin with St. John of the Cross

When it came time for the prophet Elias to be removed from this world, he asked his disciple Eliseus what he would like him to leave him. "And Eliseus said: I beseech thee that in me may be thy double spirit," desiring above all else to possess the prophet's power of apprehending supernatural as well as natural reality. Elias replied that he had "asked a hard thing: nevertheless if thou see me when I am taken from thee, thou shalt have what thou asked: but if thou see me not, thou shalt not have it." In other words, whoever recognizes the supernatural on sight, proves by that very fact that he possesses the gift commonly referred to as "a sense of the supernatural." It's that simple.

When Eliseus actually saw his master carried off the earth in a fiery chariot by a whirlwind, he knew his wish had been granted and therefore "took up the mantle of Elias that fell from him" (4Kgs. 2:9-13). He was not the last to wear it, for as our Lord told the crowds concerning St. John the Baptist, "all the prophets and the law prophesied until John, and if you will receive it, he is Elias that is to come" (Matt. 11:13-14). Like his spiritual ancestor, who was described as "a hairy man with a girdle of leather about his loins" (4Kgs. 1:8), John too "was clothed with camels' hair, and a leathern girdle about his loins" (Mk. 1:6).

Not long after the Baptist's death at the hands of Herod, Elias himself reappeared briefly at our Lord's Transfiguration on Mt. Thabor, where the Apostles Peter, James and John saw him speaking in the company of Moses. About four hundred years before that, Malachy, the last of the Old Testament prophets, had promised that God "will send you Elias the prophet, before the coming of the great and dreadful day of the Lord ... lest I come and strike the earth with anathema" (Mal. 4:5-6). On their way down from the mountain, our Lord confirmed this prediction assuring the Apostles that "Elias indeed shall come and restore all things. But I say to you that Elias is already come" giving them to understand that "he had spoken to them of John the Baptist" (Matt. 17:11-13), whose name would hereafter resound in the Church's *Confiteor.*

The multitudes had already been told publicly:

> There hath not risen among them that are born of women a greater than John the Baptist: yet he that is the lesser in the kingdom of heaven is greater than he. And from the days of John the Baptist until now, the kingdom of heaven suffereth violence, and the violent bear it away ... He that has ears to hear, let him hear! (Matt. 11:11-15).

Since that time masters of the spiritual life in the power of Elias have never been lacking to the Church. Their teaching, crystallized in that of the Desert Fathers and codified by St. Cassian, channeled its way through St. Basil and St. Benedict into both eastern and western monasticism until now, creating saints in variety and abundance.

To them we owe not only the knotted discipline and the rules of Christian asceticism, but also our blessed Lady's Rosary and Scapular. When she appeared to the Carmelite Superior General St. Simon Stock and gave him the Brown Scapular, she promised that whoever died wearing it would never suffer hellfire. If the Rosary beads she had confided earlier to St. Dominic represented the 150 Psalms recited daily by the Fathers, what was this scapular garment but the mantle of Elias, which our Lady now saw fit to throw over the shoulders of all her children? By the Rosary and the Scapular, she declared that she would one day save the world!

In direct line of descent from the mighty Elias and St. John the Baptist stands St. John of the Cross, modern reformer together with St. Teresa of Avila of the order of the "sons of the prophet," which according to ancient tradition had been founded originally by Elias on Mt. Carmel. As a religious society it is unique in that it was never designed to "do," but to "stand" continually in the sight of the Lord of hosts in the spirit of its founder. Its entire rule is summed up in one verse of the first Psalm, where the just man is described as one whose "will is in the law of the Lord, and on his law he shall meditate day and night." Its inspiration has always been attributed to our Lady, the Flower of Carmel, whom Elias beheld in the distance from the top of his mountain, rising as "a little cloud ... out of the sea like a man's foot" which grew till "there fell a great rain" on the parched earth (3Kgs. 18:45).

The spirit of Elias is one of unmitigated intransigence in the face of apostasy. His life already spanning nearly three millennia without tasting death, the prophet will die only by martyrdom in the final tribulation, for his fidelity is impregnable. "With zeal have I been zealous for the Lord God of hosts!" he told God, "before whose face I stand," in the cave on Mt. Horeb, and never has he departed from that declaration (3Kgs. 19:10;18:15). To the public called to Mt. Carmel to witness the showdown between himself and Baal's 450 priests and Jezabel's 400 prophets, St. Elias had cried out, "How long do you halt between two sides? If the Lord be God, follow him: but if Baal, then follow him!" (3Kgs.18:21). With similar lack of ambiguity, John the Baptist would speak of "laying the axe to the root of the trees" when he caught sight of the Pharisees and Sadducees coming to his baptism in the desert of Judea. "Brood of vipers!" he called them. (Matt. 3:7-10).

St. John of the Cross, a true son of the prophets, would see the spiritual life in similar terms. As he wrote to one of his penitents, "Anything apart from God is constraint!" For him, whatever is not God is *nada*, nothing at all. Reduced to one principle, his doctrine is that faith is the only proximate means of union with God in this life. Other means—vocal prayers, visions, preaching, even good works and the whole panoply of creation— can be very helpful, but have no power to reach Him except through faith. The less dependent on sensible supports faith becomes, the purer it is and the closer to its goal. Spiritual progress, in other words, is a gradual discarding of inessentials, effected by a loving, Godward groping will. There is no denial of the natural order, but an emphasis on what lies above and beyond it, which is God himself.

Vested in the mantle of the mighty prophet who "is already come" but has yet to return, St. John of the Cross prepares the individual's way to God as St. John the Baptist prepared Israel's: "Every valley shall be filled; and every mountain and hill shall be brought low; and the crooked shall be made straight; and the rough ways plain; and all flesh shall see the salvation of God" (Matt. 17:11; Luke 3:5-6). Arriving on the scene just as the Great Apostasy began breaking over the heads of the faithful, the Carmelite master directed his teaching not only to spiritual directors unacquainted with the subtleties of the mystical ascent, but to any ardent soul unable to find a good director. How much more indispensable is he today, when the enemy has actually penetrated the Church's fortifications and preempted her chains of command!

To him can be truly applied the words of the prophet Malachy, which the Gospels applied to the great Precursor, "Behold I send my angel before thy face, who shall prepare thy way before thee" (Mal. 3:1; Matt. 11:10, Mk. 1:2; Luke 1:17), for he is a sure guide for those *in via*. Whereas the Desert Fathers concentrated on man's active role in achieving sanctification with God's cooperation—sometimes even incurring accusations of semi-Pelagianism—the Carmelite master concentrates on God's role with man's passive cooperation. A Doctor of the Church, he is par excellence her mystical theologian, the approved mentor for travelers climbing the narrow way stretching from ordinary virtue to the steeper heights.

In *The Dark Night of the Soul,* which originally formed part of *The Ascent of Mt. Carmel,* the saint explains that there are:

> ... two kinds of darkness or purgation corresponding to the two parts of man's nature—namely, the sensual and the spiritual. And thus the one night or purgation will be sensual, wherein the soul is purged according to sense, which is subdued to the spirit; and the other is a night or purgation which is spiritual, wherein the soul is purged and stripped according to the spirit and subdued and made ready for the union of love with God. The night of sense is

common and comes to many: these are the beginners ... The night of the spirit is the portion of very few.

St. John of the Cross does not, therefore, address the gross sinner in need of conversion, but the man in the parable who finds his house "swept and garnished" after being vacated by the unclean spirit and now threatened by seven other spirits worse than the first one (Luke 11:24-26). As the parable makes clear, a second conversion is necessary to reach sanctity, for mere natural perfection, although good in itself, unfortunately provides the foundation for truly enormous sins found only in souls sufficiently practiced in virtue to pass for "good" in their own eyes and even in the eyes of others. In other words, the seven (or maybe eight) spirits who take over the well swept soul represent the seven capital sins in spiritual guise, deadlier by far than the common variety.

Reversing the order in which the Desert Fathers tackled them, St. John of the Cross begins where the Fathers ended, with the hellish one underlying and actuating all the others. He starts with the sin which is the devil's very own, the primordial sin of...

Pride

People serious about the spiritual life are not likely to fall into the more obvious forms of pride. Like the Pharisee standing at prayer in the Temple in the parable, they are truly "not as the rest of men ... as also is this publican" (Luke 18:11). Having acquired considerable mastery over their sensual inclinations and a degree of detachment from material possessions, they are, so to speak, accustomed to "fast twice in a week" and "give tithes of all they possess." Finding their highest satisfactions in spiritual accomplishments, they are drawn to thank God not for mere temporal benefits, but for the fact that they are not "extortioners, unjust, adulterers."

Persons so afflicted are blissfully unaware of their condition, for blindness is integral to pride. A master psychotherapist in both the natural and the supernatural order, St. John of the Cross therefore begins by diagnosing the problem. He says:

> As these beginners feel themselves to be very fervent and diligent in spiritual things and devout exercises ... there often comes to them, through their imperfections, a certain kind of secret pride, whence they come to have some degree of satisfaction with their works and with themselves.

Approaching this deadly vice as he would a life-threatening disease, he lists some telltale symptoms by which it betrays its presence. Watch out first of all, says he, for "a certain desire, which is somewhat vain, and at times very vain, to speak of spiritual things in the presence of others," preferring to teach rather than to learn.

This is an occupational hazard for new converts. Because of their extreme weakness, God normally grants beginners in the spiritual combat lights and consolations not usually accorded to veterans. Glorying in their sudden prosperity, their behavior is not unlike that of the *nouveau riche* enjoying overnight financial success. Believing themselves to be specially favored, they appoint themselves gurus to those more ignorant than themselves, all the while not hesitating to instruct others who may in fact be far advanced in the ways of God. Condemning their fellows in their hearts for not having "the kind of devotion which they themselves desire," they even go so far in their blind inexperience as to criticize them openly for their deficiencies.

The mystical doctor cautions that the devil often increases the fervor of neophytes in performing good works, so as to swell their pride and presumption even more. "For the devil knows quite well that all these works and virtues ... are not only valueless to them, but *even become vices in them,"* like the fasts and tithes of the benighted Pharisee. Seeking out spiritual guides who will tell them what they want to hear, they steer clear "as they would from death" of those who do not approve of the direction their piety may be taking, or who try to correct them, convinced that such confessors "do not understand them or ... are themselves not spiritual. ... Presuming thus," notes the saint wryly, "they are wont to resolve much and accomplish very little."

And all this amid considerable trumpet blowing, for an insistent urge to play to the grandstand is also evident, to others if not to themselves.

> Anxious that others shall realize how spiritual and devout they are ... they occasionally give outward evidence thereof in movements, sighs and other ceremonies; and at times they are apt to fall into ecstasies, in public rather than in secret, wherein the devil aids them, and they are pleased that this should be noticed, and are often eager that this should be noticed more.

Who could fail to detect manifestations of spiritual pride in the charismatic excesses and false apparitions currently plaguing the Church?

Even if not expressed openly, the need to be "special," to be their confessor's favorite, drives many into envy and disquiet the moment they feel they may not be "teacher's pet." In the confessional, those so afflicted customarily minimize their sins, says the saint, "too much embarrassed to confess them nakedly lest their confessors think less of them" and go so far on occasion as to "seek another confessor to tell the wrongs they have done, so that their own confessor shall think they have done nothing wrong at all." St. John says, "It is to excuse themselves rather than to accuse themselves that they go to confession ... thus they always take pleasure in telling him what is good, and sometimes in such terms as to make it appear to be greater than it is." In his day the "reconciliation room" for face-to-face confessions was unheard of, especially for hearing the confessions of women. What he would think of such a theater of operations can be imagined.

Anger and impatience with one's faults are also commonly found in beginners, who make little of them at one moment only to fall into despondency over them at the next.

> Often they beseech God with great yearnings that He will take from them their imperfections and faults, but they do this that they may find themselves at peace, and may not be troubled by them,

rather than for God's sake; not realizing that if He should take their imperfections from them, they would probably become prouder and more presumptuous still. They dislike praising others and love to be praised themselves; sometimes they seek out such praise. Herein they are like the foolish virgins who, when their lamps could not be lit, sought oil from others.

If these imperfections are not recognized and remedied in time, "some souls go on to develop many very grave ones which do them great harm. But some have fewer and some more, and some only the first motions thereof or little beyond these." During times of fervor, however, "there are hardly any such beginners who ... fall not into some of these errors." Even after reaching a certain proficiency in the spiritual life, the saint warns that they must always contend with the old *hebetudo mentis* bequeathed by original sin and "the natural roughness which every man contracts through sin and the distraction and outward clinging of the spirit."

Emboldened by their own fidelity to prayer, they may treat too familiarly with God. Rushing in where angels fear to tread, they fail in the proper respect and courtesy, "such as a soul must ever observe in converse with the Most High." (363) Even the great lawgiver Moses had to be commanded by God to stand back and remove his shoes before addressing Him at the burning bush, whereas in later life, after much experience in the ways of God, he would not dare to draw near or look at Him. St. Peter likewise, made aware of God's power at close quarters during the miraculous draught of fishes, fell to his knees and could only exclaim, "Depart from me, for I am a sinful man, O Lord!" (Luke 5:8).

Human beings normally become more familiar in their prolonged dealings with one another, but the exact reverse proves true in their dealings with God. Natural instinct leads us to expect that perseverance in prayer renders relations with heaven ever more casual and relaxed, but hagiography proves that prayer only increases our sense of unworthiness. If it does not, there is something amiss, for the greatest saints have always ended by believing themselves to be the greatest sinners. Truly holy people are not those who crowd about the altar or experiment with the sacred liturgy. There is in fact no surer indication of shallow spirituality than a chummy familiarity with God or His representatives, for God himself teaches us humility when we come near Him. In our day, which has seen sacrilege perpetrated at every level of worship, St. John's words speak volumes.

Unfortunately God's highest graces can serve to feed pride, for souls favored with divine consolations beyond the ordinary are specially liable to develop a craving for God which is "somewhat bolder than fitting, and discourteous and ill-considered." Recipients of genuine spiritual communications often fall prey to the deceits of the devil, who "causes many to believe in vain visions and false prophecies and strives to make them presume that God and the saints are speaking with them, and they often trust their own fancy." Filled with pride, "they become bold with God and lose holy fear, which is the key and custodian of all the virtues; and in some of these souls so many are the falsehoods and deceits which tend to multiply, and so inveterate do they grow, that it is very doubtful if such souls will return to the pure road of virtue and true spirituality."

St. John describes very differently those few souls destined to reach perfection by way of humility. They,

> ...think naught of their own affairs ... having very little satisfaction with themselves; they consider all others as far better, and usually have a holy envy of them and an eagerness to serve God as they do ... The more do they realize how much God deserves of them, and how little is all they do for His sake ... the less they are satisfied ... If men should praise and esteem them, they can in no wise believe what they say. These souls have a deep desire to be taught by anyone who can bring them profit; they are the complete opposite of those of whom we have spoken above, who would fain be always teaching, and who, when others seem to be teaching them, take the words from their mouths as if they knew them already.

Rejoicing to hear others praised, the humble

...are more anxious to speak of their faults and sins, or that these should be recognized rather than their virtues ... This is characteristic of the spirit which is simple, pure, genuine and very pleasing to God. For as the wise Spirit of God dwells in these humble souls, He ... inclines them to keep His treasures secretly within, and likewise to cast out from themselves all evil. But souls who in the beginning journey with this kind of perfection are ... a minority, and very few are those who ... do not fall into the opposite errors.

For ordinary souls, prayer and humiliations are the usual remedy, but those whom God desires to purify from all these imperfections, St. John says will be led into the "nights." And with that he proceeds to treat of the second of the capital sins in spiritual guise, which is ...

Avarice

Here again, people who think of themselves as "good" are addressed, who believe that because they are preoccupied with the things of God, are by the same token godly. St. John is therefore at pains to show how the spiritually avaricious, like the spiritually proud, deceive both themselves and others by taking pleasure in legitimate things which are occasions of sin for them.

What is avarice? An inordinate desire to possess.

To bring the hidden malice of this deadly vice into full view, our Lord told us to "behold the birds of the air" and "consider the lilies of the field," and to mark how God feeds and clothes the one and the other, although the birds "do not reap, nor gather into barns" and the lilies "labor not, neither do they spin." And He asks, "Are you not of much more value than they?" This being the case, "Be not solicitous therefore, saying, What shall we eat: or what shall we drink, or wherewith shall we be clothed? ... For your Father knoweth that you have need of all these things."

He points out that things are what "the heathens seek." The redeemed are expected to operate according to a radically different agenda, for as long as they continue to "seek ... first the kingdom of God and his justice," all their necessities are automatically supplied. "Therefore I say to you, be not solicitous for your life, what you shall eat, nor for your body, what you shall put on. Is not the life more than the meat: and the body more than the raiment?" (Matt. 6:25-34). This passage in Scripture not only defines the basic law underlying world economics and every domestic budget; it reveals that the essence of avarice does not lie in possessions or even in the love of possessions. After all, like us, birds must eat and lilies be clothed, and there is no sin in that.

As the Desert Fathers pointed out, the specific malice of avarice lies in mistrust of God. Instead of resting securely in Him and His unfailing Providence, fallen human nature seeks reassurance by taking refuge in things. Adam and Eve, bereft of loving trust in their Creator as a consequence of their disobedience, immediately "hid themselves from the face of the Lord God amidst the trees of paradise," hoping to conceal their nakedness behind creatures lower than themselves. Thus hoping to obfuscate what we really are by what we have, we succeed only in placing obstacles between ourselves and God, who must call, "Where art thou?" (Gen. 4:8-9) as He did to Adam, to bring us out into the open to speak with Him.

If our Lord prefaces His little parable about the birds and the lilies by saying that natural life is "more than the meat," it follows that the supernatural life is greater than the natural, and spiritual avarice deadlier by far than its common form. In what may be called the "well-swept" soul, ordinary greed rises to a higher plane, where inordinate possessions and attachments figure as indispensable adjuncts to spiritual progress. Many of the spiritually greedy "can never have enough of listening to counsels and learning spiritual precepts," says St. John, "and of possessing and reading many books which treat of this matter, and they spend their time on all these things rather than on works of mortification and the perfecting of the inward poverty of spirit which should be theirs."

This unfortunately does not preclude attachments to material objects, for "they burden themselves with images and rosaries which are very curious and showy," and today it's not unlikely that some of the latter may have allegedly turned to gold at some apparition site. "Now they put down one, now take up another; now they change about, now change back again; now they want this kind of thing, now that, preferring one kind of cross to another because it is more curious. And others you will see adorned ... like children with trinkets."

To believe that such things cannot possibly feed avarice because they are sacramentals of the Church is a grievous error, easily proved when the owner refuses to part with them should the occasion arise. St. John cites two cases in point from his own experience, one,

> ...a person who for more than ten years made use of a cross roughly formed from a branch that had been blessed, fastened with a pin twisted round it. He had never ceased using it, and he always carried it about with him until I took it from him, and this was a person of no small sense and understanding! And I saw another who said his prayers using beads that were made of bones from the spine of a fish, [although] these things carried no devotion in their workmanship or value.

These illustrations show that what we are attached to doesn't have to be expensive or remarkable in any way to feed avarice. We only have to be attached to it. Nor is the mania for collecting limited to objects, for it extends to people as well, especially to people who seem to offer spiritual security. As St. John notes, one of the characteristics of the spiritually greedy is habitual discontent with the spirituality God gives them, being "very disconsolate and querulous because they find not in spiritual things the consolation that they would desire." An outstanding manifestation of this distemper in our day is to be found in the endless "dialogues" and conferences which effectively prevent progress in the spiritual life by keeping everyone talking about problems meant to be suffered rather than solved, or which do not concern them.

All the while condemning spiritual avarice, which in advanced souls can persist even in attachment to supernatural visions, St. John makes it clear that he is no iconoclast. He says:

Here it must be borne in mind that this doctrine of ours does not agree, nor do we desire that it should agree, with the doctrine of those pestilent men who, inspired by Satanic pride and envy, have desired to remove from the eyes of the faithful the holy and necessary use and the worthy adoration [in the sense of veneration] of images of God and of the saints. This teaching of ours is very different from that; for we say not here, as they do, that images should not exist and should not be adored; we simply explain the difference between images and God.

The faithful have had much to suffer from the "pestilent men" mentioned above, who in our day have stripped Catholic altars and chapels of statues and pictures and reduced so many churches to meetinghouses. The best we can do is make a virtue of necessity, keeping in mind St. Paul's assurance that all things work unto good for those who really love God. Perhaps He is using this means to make us grow in spiritual poverty, to which avarice of any kind is so irreducible an obstacle. That we of our own strength can never eradicate our spiritual sins is the *leitmotiv* running through all St. John's works. We may lop off the tops of the weeds, but only God can pull the roots, and He does so by introducing us into the bitter privation of the dark nights.

For means are good and necessary to an end, and images are means which serve to remind us of God and of the saints. But when we consider and attend more than is necessary for treating them as such, they disturb and hinder us as much, in their own way, as any different thing ... Provided the soul pays no more heed to them than is necessary ... they will ever assist it to union with God, allowing the soul to soar upwards, when God grants that favor, from the superficial image to the living God, forgetting every creature and everything that belongs to creatures.

When our Lord said, "Be not solicitous," He issued a positive commandment. To disregard it is to fall headlong into avarice, the capital sin directly contrary to hope, whose importance cannot be overestimated, for it is one of the three theological virtues indispensable for reaching God. All possession is contrary to hope and weakens it, inasmuch as we cannot hope for what we have, but only for what we have not; and what we have not in this life is the Beatific Vision. For this should be our craving, the mouth of desire, as St. John wrote to the nuns of Beas, ever open towards God alone.

And so, "We exhort men to pass beyond that which is superficial that they may not be hindered from attaining to the living truth beneath it, and to make no more account of the former than suffices for attainment to the spiritual." The avaricious man is called a miser, because the proper end of avarice is misery, a life apart from God. He has become so insecure he cannot bear to part with anything, even for his own use and well-being, and dies on a mattress stuffed with wealth.

On the other hand,

> Those who make good progress attach themselves to no visible instruments, nor do they burden themselves with such, nor desire to know more than is necessary in order that they may act well; for they set their eyes only on being right with God and on pleasing Him, and therein consists their covetousness. And thus with great generosity they give away all that they have, and delight to know that they have it not, for God's sake and for charity to their neighbor, no matter whether these be spiritual things or temporal. For, as I say, they set their eyes only upon the reality of interior perfection, which is to give pleasure to God and in naught to give pleasure to themselves.

Through His Psalmist He told us, "Open thy mouth wide, and *I* will fill it!" (Ps. 80:11).

Having disposed of spiritual avarice, St. John proceeds to treat of the third capital sin in spiritual guise, which in his day was politely referred to as luxury, but which we call lechery or...

Lust

Because the world at large concerns itself only with the carnal aspects of this sin, few Christians are prepared to look for it in their devotions. Until they learn otherwise, those seriously committed to a life of prayer and making progress in virtue may be tempted to believe that true piety automatically excludes "that sort of thing." That St. John of the Cross actually dwells more at length on the spiritual forms of this vice than on those of the other capital sins may therefore come as a surprise. Long before Freud, however, he discerned the many disguises wayward sexuality is wont to assume to curry favor with the godly and pass itself off as a fruit of charity.

Church history yields many sad examples of the sexual aberrations of the devout, ranging from those of the early Messalians to those of Fr. Molinos and his Quietists, on down to the antics of modern revivalists and holy rollers who spend a deal of their worship time on the floor. Sex and prayer are in fact rather close traveling companions, due to the fact that by their very nature both are ordered to a *union with persons,* carnal in one instance and divine in the other. Human nature, fallen and befuddled by sin as it is, therefore easily confuses the two.

Meeting with the good Pharisee Nicodemus by night, our Lord was at pains to explain to him how the two orders of reality, the earthly and the heavenly, although found together in this life, do not produce the same effects and must not be mistaken one for the other: "That which is born of the flesh is flesh; and that which is born of the Spirit is spirit" (John 3:6). St. Paul would go on to explain, "Now the works of the flesh are manifest, which are fornication, uncleanness, immodesty, luxury ... But the fruit of the Spirit is charity ... modesty, continency, chastity" (Gal. 5:19,22).

Days St. John of the Cross:

> And thus, with respect to this sin of luxury, [beginners] have many imperfections which might be described as spiritual luxury, not because they are so, but because the imperfections proceed from spiritual things. For it often comes to pass that in their very spiritual exercises, when they are powerless to prevent it, there arise and assert themselves in the sensual part of the soul impure acts and motions, and sometimes this happens even when the spirit is deep in prayer, or engaged in the Sacrament of Penance or in the Eucharist.

The holy doctor finds these imperfections actually stem from three causes, the first and most important of which is *the natural pleasure which our human nature takes in spiritual things.* This is unavoidable, because spiritual pleasure easily overflows into sense, which responds in the only way it can in accordance with the nature God gave it. It gets into the act, as it were, in order to take what it can for itself, "for when the spirit and the sense are pleased, every part of a man is moved by that pleasure to delight according to its proportion and nature.

> For then the spirit, which is the higher part, is moved to pleasure and delight in God; and the sensual nature, which is the lower part, is moved to pleasure and delight of the senses, because it cannot possess and lay hold on anything else, so it lays hold on what is nearest to itself, which is impure and sensual. Thus it happens that the soul is in deep prayer with God according to the spirit, and on the other hand, according to the senses it is passively conscious (not without displeasure) of rebellions and motions and acts of the senses.

He mentions that this is most likely to occur at the time of Holy Communion.

Little or no harm is done as long as this uninvited sensuality remains uninvited and is clearly recognized as the distraction it is, to be ignored as much as possible. The damage comes from mistaking it for spirituality and holiness, or worse still, as union with God. The spiritually immature may believe themselves to be in ecstasy, whereas they are actually prey to an experience commonly produced under the revival tent. What is born of the flesh is flesh; of itself it can never rise into the spirit or become spirit. To think so lies at the base of modern naturalism, one of whose rampant heresies is an unhealthy glorification of sex, even in marriage.

Well aware of the charismatic excesses of his day which filtered into the Church from the pagan Dionysian rites, St. Paul never tired of exhorting those "risen with Christ" to "seek the things that are above" (Col. 3:1) and to rest no longer than necessary in their spiritual beginnings, where flesh plays so large a part. *God cannot be reached through the senses.* Trying to do so was the specific sin of the men who built Babel and began a tower, "the top whereof may reach heaven" (Gen. 11:4). St. John of the Cross was adamant in teaching that faith alone is the proportionate and proximate means to God. Even love goes nowhere without faith. Nor do the Sacraments. Although making use of sensible signs, they confer grace only through the faith of the Church and their recipients. How many times did our Lord say, after some miraculous cure "Thy faith has saved thee!" And how often could He perform no miracles where faith in Him was lacking?

The second cause of spiritual lust according to the mystical doctor is *the devil*, who sometimes succeeds in making fervent souls abandon prayer by stirring up impurity. He has two reasons for doing this, the first of which is to make them so fearful of impure motions that they become reluctant to give themselves to prayer.

> He succeeds in portraying to them very vividly things which are most foul and impure, and at times are closely related to certain spiritual things and persons that are of profit to their souls, in order to terrify them and make them fearful; so that those who are affected by this dare not even look at anything or meditate upon anything, because they immediately encounter this temptation ... When these impurities attack such souls through the medium of melancholy [the saint is speaking here of persons neurotically inclined] they are not as a rule freed from them until they have been cured of that kind of humour, unless the dark night has entered the soul and rids them of all impurities one after the other.

Meanwhile, they must do battle.

The devil's second reason in exciting lust is to divert his victims into moral aberrations, fascinating and deluding them by his misrepresentations. Diabolically inspired was Priscillianism, whose adherents even reached the point of worshiping in the nude in the name of God and innocence. The whole panoply of Catharism hatched by the Manichees suffered like delusions, which in St. John's own day were found among the Illuminists.

The third cause of spiritual lust is undue fear of sexual motions in ourselves, which arouse the very reactions we dread.

As Job said, "For the fear which I feared hath come upon me: and that which I was afraid of hath befallen me!" (3:25). Modern psychology will bear out St. John's warning that fear can generate obsession, even hallucinations of the thing feared.

> There are also certain souls of so tender and frail a nature that when there comes to them some spiritual consolation or some grace in prayer, the spirit of luxury is with them immediately, inebriating and delighting their sensual nature in such manner that it is as if they were plunged into the enjoyment and pleasure of this sin; and the enjoyment remains, together with the consolation, passively, and sometimes they are able to see that certain impure and unruly acts have taken place ... and the same thing happens to such souls when they are enkindled with anger or suffer any disturbance or grief.

In other words, there are persons who are not altogether accountable for their feelings, being constitutionally hyper-emotional.

Outside prayer the symptoms of spiritual lust are more subtly manifested and not readily detected. There are two, however, which betray the underlying malady. St. John says spiritual persons must learn to recognize "a certain bravado in speaking or performing spiritual actions with respect to certain persons present." This is a form of exhibitionism which is sexual in its source in that it desires vain gratification from those to whom we happen to be attracted. It is like the antics of the little boy showing off before the girl he has a crush on. The action itself is not impure, but the subconscious desire is which prompts it. Spiritual persons do this spiritually, to impress others they consider spiritual.

The second symptom is found, not surprisingly, in the area of friendships which we sincerely believe to be spiritual, but which nevertheless often take their rise from lust.

Says St. John:

> This may be known to be the case when the remembrance of the friendship causes not the love of God to grow, but occasions remorse of conscience. For when the friendship is purely spiritual,

the love of God grows with it; and the more the soul remembers it, the more it remembers the love of God and the greater the desire it has for God; so that, as the one grows, the other grows also. For the spirit of God has this property, that it increases good by adding to it more good, inasmuch as there is likeness and conformity between them. But when this love arises from the vice of sensuality it produces contrary effects, for the more the one grows, the more the other decreases.

The test of a true spiritual friendship is therefore quite simple:

Does it cause the love of God to grow in us? Does it cause our sensuality to decrease?

Does remembrance of it cause twinges of conscience?

"If that sensual love grows, it will at once be observed that the soul's love for God is becoming colder, and that it is forgetting Him as it remembers that love; there comes to it, too, a certain remorse of conscience." In other words, as in all spiritual sins, God is not the main object, but only made an excuse for self indulgence. Many a religious vocation has foundered on this reef. "And on the other hand, if the love of God grows in the soul, that other love becomes cold and forgotten; for, as the two are contrary to one another, not only does the one not aid the other, but the one which predominates quenches and confounds the other."

As our Lord said, "That which is born of the flesh is flesh, and that which is born of the Spirit is spirit." Persons faithful to God progressively "outgrow" human associations which do not contribute to divine union. If they do not find them actually dangerous, they find them insipid, and useless. St. John would say "vain." He promises that love of God will eventually put an end to all carnal friendships. In the purgative night, both natural and supernatural loves are brought under control, for "it strengthens and purifies the one ... according to God, and the other it brings to an end," after causing them both to be lost sight of for a while.

And that brings us to the next consideration, which is that of spiritual...

Anger

When it comes to understanding human complexes and our ability to rationalize, St. John of the Cross not only ranks with the Desert Fathers, but by virtue of the supernatural dimension he brings to his diagnoses, he far outranks modern psychologists. If the world appreciates him so little, it is because his ministry was charismatic in the true sense of the word, exercised in charity for the benefit of souls without worldly ambitions. The remedies he prescribes depend much more on God than on men.

As we have seen, the Desert Fathers were aware that anger is both a passion and a sin and can be indulged in justly, as did our Lord when He drove the money-changers from the Temple. What was true with Him, however, is rarely the case with disordered human nature. Because anger when it erupts unsettles the reason, the angry man always thinks his anger just, being unable to think clearly while in its throes. As we have seen, this is why the Desert Fathers and other great masters of the spiritual life have laid down as a general rule never to give vent to anger under any circumstances, no matter how justified it may appear at the moment.

Our Lord clearly demonstrated the connection between anger and the Fifth Commandment when He reminded His listeners after the Sermon on the Mount, "You have heard that it was said to them of old: Thou shalt not kill. And whosoever shall kill shall be in danger of the judgment. But I say to you that whosoever is angry with his brother shall be in danger of the judgment" (Matt. 5:21-22), for the proper end of anger, if allowed to run its full course, is the extermination of the adversary. Like all vices, it is a usurpation of the rights of God, who in this regard lays down, "Revenge is mine. I will repay!" (Rom. 12:19)

Anger is especially dangerous in spiritual form, for it masquerades easily as righteous indignation, aroused for the glory of God. We all know how many wars have been fought in the name of religion. St. John of the Cross' treatment of the aberration is brief, but to the point. In his exposition of *The*

Spiritual Canticle he defines wrath as "a certain impetuosity that disturbs peace, going beyond the limits thereof," and elsewhere (in the Canticle's first edition) as "a certain impetuosity that goes beyond the limit of reason when it works viciously." It is a deadly enemy of prayer, which above all requires peace and tranquility if it is to thrive.

Like the Desert Fathers the mystical doctor saw clearly that anger is not primarily rooted in the object of its displeasure, but in frustration, i.e., in concupiscence. In this regard spiritual anger is no different from its carnal forms. Because the passion is a defensive one, abruptly aroused to acquire what we want and are not getting, or to ward off something we do not want and are getting, spiritual anger can be expected to manifest itself whenever the hunger for spiritual consolation is thwarted and desolation sets in. Rushing by its very nature toward gratification and flying from the Cross, anger can be directed against God as well as against our neighbor.

To diagnose the distemper quickly, St. John would have us look for three major symptoms: Speaking of souls of prayer whom God is weaning from their early fervors, he writes, "When their delight and pleasure in spiritual things come to an end, they naturally become embittered, and bear that lack of sweetness with a bad grace." There are immediate and visible repercussions in their outward lives, for their sudden sense of deprivation "affects all they do; and they very easily become irritated over the smallest matter. Sometimes, indeed, none can tolerate them."

"This frequently happens after they have been very pleasantly recollected according to sense; when their pleasure and delight therein come to an end, their nature is naturally vexed and disappointed, just as is the child when they take it from the breast of which it was enjoying the sweetness." As in ordinary anger, "There is no sin in this natural vexation, when it is not permitted to indulge itself, but only imperfection." If allowed to persist, however, it can throw the whole spiritual life off balance, for it is a clear indication that God is being sought in prayer, not for himself, but only for His gifts. The next symptom to watch for is untoward irritation at the sins of others, supposedly motivated by charitable zeal. "At times the impulse comes to them to reprove them angrily, and occasionally they go so far as to indulge it and set themselves up as masters of virtue. All this is contrary to spiritual meekness." And also, we might add, fed more than a little by pride.

Modern psychology has contributed its bit by elaborating on this well known human tendency to be angry at what others do, even though their actions may not concern us directly. It has defined as "projection" the mechanism whereby we alleviate guilt by accusing others of our own failings. The ancients were well aware of this subterfuge of the subconscious, for many an ascetical manual recommends examining our consciences for the faults we find particularly obnoxious in others, in order to detect the very ones to which we are blind in our regard. If these did not lurk in the recesses of our own souls, we could never recognize their manifestations so quickly in others, nor would we be so intransigent in wishing to correct them.

The third big symptom to watch for is undue impatience with our own imperfections. Irascible temperaments want everything done yesterday, and once they have made up their minds to become saints, they naturally expect to do so overnight, believing as often as not that their impatience is some kind of humility.

Says St. John:

> Many of these persons purpose to accomplish a great deal and make grand resolutions, yet, as they are not humble and have no misgivings about themselves, the more resolutions they make, the greater is their fall and the greater their annoyance, since they have not the patience to wait for that which God will give them when it pleases Him.

Patience is anger's contrary, and as St. Teresa of Avila's bookmark reads "*La paciencia todo alcanze.*" It is a virtue which can accomplish anything in due time. Her co-reformer of Carmel was not noted for a runaway sense of humor, and on occasion she was known to twit him for taking everything dead seriously. At the close of the foregoing admonition on anger, however, even he could not forbear adding, "Some souls, on the other hand, are so patient as regards the progress which they desire that God would gladly see them less so!" Leading us to suspect that a little anger is not altogether a dangerous thing.

Comes the next sin in spiritual guise, the well known...

Gluttony

As we have seen, anger springs from the frustration of some craving.

The next sin on St. John's list is in many ways its exact opposite, for it attacks us, not when our wants are frustrated, but when our wants are being satisfied. Anger and gluttony therefore maintain a subtle underground connection, so that we tend to oscillate between the two, depending on how things are going for us. Mother Eve, who was created free of all concupiscence and lacked for nothing in the Garden of Eden, could not fall prey to anger, but fell prey to gluttony because, like the glorious Lucifer, she wanted even more of the good things she already had.

The Desert Fathers rested the entire moral life on the control of this inordinate desire for what appears good, not only "good to eat," but "fair to the eyes and delightful to behold" (Gen. 3:6). That St. John says "there is much to be said" about gluttony should therefore come as no surprise. He explores its spiritual ramifications as thoroughly as those of pride and lust. Pride may be the key to the intellect, but gluttony is the key to the will, which is a blind faculty ever groping for what it wants. Well acquainted with human psychology, the devil did not begin tempting our Lord in the desert by offering Him the whole world right off; he began with the gambit which worked so successfully with Eve, by suggesting He satisfy His natural hunger by extraordinary means.

"If thou be the Son of God," said he cunningly, "command that these stones be made into bread." To which the Incarnate Truth replies with a verse from Scripture saying, "Not in bread alone doth man live, but in every word that proceedeth from the mouth of God" (Matt. 4:3-4). Although carnal food is indispensable if the body is to live, our Lord lays down before beginning His public ministry that spiritual food is even more necessary if the soul which animates the body is to live. Fundamentally, this is the basic human need for God, which in fallen nature automatically gives rise to avidity for spiritual consolations. The specific malice of this vice is similar to that of lust, for whereas lust puts pleasure above the procreation of society, gluttony puts pleasure above the nourishment of the individual.

St. John says there is almost no beginner in prayer who doesn't fall into this imperfection. At first God deliberately uses the pleasure derived from spiritual food to wean us from the pleasures of the world, but unless the desire for it is curbed and eventually brought under control, the whole spiritual edifice founders. Union with God, who is spirit and beyond all sense, can never be effected by sensual, psychological means of any kind, no matter how "spiritual" it may seem. As our Lord told the Samaritan woman at the well, "The hour is coming, and is now here, when the true worshipers will worship the Father in spirit and in truth. For the Father also seeks such to worship him. God is spirit, and they who worship him must worship in spirit and in truth."

Nothing happens by chance in Scripture, and it's noteworthy that our Lord initiated this memorable conversation by asking the woman for a drink of water, prolonging it while His disciples had gone into town for food. This story deals with bedrock fundamentals, for when the disciples returned they "prayed him, saying, 'Rabbi, eat.' But he said to them, 'I have meat to eat which you know not. ... My meat is to do the will of him that sent me, that I may perfect his work'" (John 4:31,34) A variation on the doctrine cited to the devil in the desert, our Lord wished His disciples to understand that our most sustaining food is invisible. It must be chosen above all others, and even if we don't like the taste, it must be partaken of gratefully and not greedily, as God gives it, in the quantity He gives it and when He gives it.

Among the signs of spiritual gluttony described by St. John, the first may surprise us, for it is rarely, if ever, encountered in our post-conciliar days when fasting has to all practical purposes disappeared and the discipline and the hair shirt have been relegated to museums. It is over-indulgence in bodily penances. Perhaps it can claim some kinship to the intoxicating "high" experienced by runners who push themselves to the limit, for the saint says that some persons so addicted,

> ...attracted by pleasure ... kill themselves with penances, and others weaken themselves with fasts by performing more than their frailty can bear, without the order or advice of any ... Inasmuch as all extremes are vicious, and as in behaving thus such persons are working their own will, they grow in vice rather than in virtue ... And many of these the devil assails, stirring up this gluttony in them through the pleasures and desires which he increases within them.

St. John continues:

> You will find that many of these persons are very insistent with their spiritual masters to be granted what they desire, extracting it from them almost by force; if they be refused it they become as peevish as children and go about in great displeasure, thinking that they are not serving God when they are not allowed to do that which they would ... Clinging to their own will and pleasure, which they treat as though it came from God ... these persons think that their own satisfaction and pleasure are the satisfaction and service of God.

Pinpointed as a major aberration is the gluttony specifically directed towards the Holy Eucharist. In the saint's time Church discipline was strict, and permission for frequent Communion had to be sought from the confessor, so that he decries those who "know so little of their own unworthiness and misery and have thrust so far from them the loving fear and reverence which they owe to the greatness of God, that they hesitate not to insist continually that their confessors shall allow them to communicate often." Not scrupling to communicate without permission, they also "make their confessions carelessly, being more eager to eat than to eat cleanly and perfectly, although it would be healthier and holier for them had they the contrary inclination."

He deems this boldness "a thing that does great harm, and men may fear to be punished for such temerity!" One shudders at what he might say of the consecrated Bread and circuses currently offered to open crowds of mixed faiths in recent post-conciliar times, when even among the faithful, receiving Holy Communion has become little more than polite routine. Spiritual gluttony on such a scale surpasses the wildest deviations of the past, when every communicant was still aware that in this Sacrament of sacraments, God himself is given under sensible appearances to be our sustenance forever. What consequences must gluttony which takes God himself for its object reap for its perpetrators?

St. John, who was concerned with devout souls who, although very imperfect, were far from outright sacrilege, goes on to say:

> These persons, in communicating, strive with every nerve to obtain some kind of sensible sweetness and pleasure, instead of humbly doing reverence and giving praise within themselves to God. And in such wise do they devote themselves to this that, when they have received no pleasure or sweetness in the senses, they think they have accomplished nothing at all.

Patients urged by their psychiatrists to "get in touch with their feelings" can therefore be certain such a practice, whatever it accomplishes, will never put them in touch with God. They will only succeed in subjecting their soul to their body and its cravings. Those who so indulge themselves St. Paul called "enemies of the cross of Christ ... whose god is their belly" (Phil. 3:18-19).

Their attitude is "completely opposed to the nature of God," says St. John, and amounts to *"impurity in faith."* They:

> ...judge God very unworthily; they have not realized that the least of the benefits which come from this Most Holy Sacrament is that which concerns the senses; and that the invisible part of the grace that it bestows is much greater; for, in order that they may

look at It with the eyes of faith, God oftentimes withholds from them these other consolations and sweetnesses of sense.

Given that the soul is faithful in its commitment, such a deprivation spells progress rather than reprehension.

Spiritual gluttons betray similar defects in regard to prayer, with other lamentable consequences. Constantly straining for sensible fervor, "wearying and fatiguing their faculties and their heads," they end by losing:

> ...true devotion and spirituality, which consist in perseverance, together with patience and humility and mistrust of themselves, that they may please God alone. For this reason, when they have once failed to find pleasure in this or some other exercise, they have great disinclination and repugnance to return to it, and at times abandon it.

Like the spiritually avaricious, but motivated primarily by sensuality:

> Such persons ... never tire, therefore, of reading books; and they begin now one meditation, now another, in their pursuit of this pleasure which they desire to experience in the things of God. But God very justly, wisely and lovingly, denies it to them, for otherwise this spiritual gluttony and inordinate appetite would breed innumerable evils.

Eventually they must enter the nights, "that they may be purged of this childishness."

St. John concludes by exposing a last imperfection common in such souls, but which he singles out as "very great," for it is calculated to undermine the whole edifice of the Christian life. As he explains it, this failing consists in "that they are very weak and remiss in journeying upon the hard road of the Cross; for the soul that is given to sweetness naturally has its face set against all self-denial, which is devoid of sweetness."

Spiritual gluttony spawns countless other faults, which he omits mentioning "lest I become too lengthy," but whatever they may be,

...spiritual temperance and sobriety lead to another and a very different temper, which is that of mortification, fear and submission in all things. It thus becomes clear that the perfection and worth of things consist not in the multitude and the pleasantness of one's actions, but in being able to deny oneself in them.

Why should prayer be an exception?

Needless to say, this advice applies all the more to avidity for visions and supernatural experiences, into which the devil so easily injects his deceits. The Johannine rule in their regard is categorical: *Renounce them all without exception.* "For, by the rejection of evil visions, the errors of the devil are avoided, and by the rejection of good visions no hindrance is offered to faith, and still the spirit harvests the fruit of them." In other words, authentic visions of which God is the author cannot be avoided in any case, and they will accomplish their work in the soul whether they are accepted or not, but they do it all the better the more we are detached from them. "If they be not rejected, they are a hindrance to the spirit, for the soul rests in them and its spirit soars not to the invisible." Whoever becomes attached to them will grow in pride, lose their full effect and eventually forfeit such favors.

"Hastening on with my account of these imperfections," St. John lumps the last two spiritual sins together, disposing of both with the utmost brevity in one short chapter. The first of them is...

Envy

As previously noted, envy is nowhere to be found among the principal sins listed by the Desert Fathers, who rested content with viewing it as a necessary concomitant of pride and vanity. That they accorded it no special classification of its own, however, cannot be taken to mean they intended to minimize it, for Scripture tells us that it was by its means, on the part of the devil, that evil entered the world in the first place. Roused to revolt on learning that God would become Man and subject him and all angelic creation to a Sacred Humanity born of a woman, Lucifer spitefully transmitted to Adam and Eve his own resentment against God, which broke out almost immediately in their children.

Ask. St. Basil:

> What urged the devil, the beginner of evil, to wage fierce war against man? Was it not envy? It was through envy he came to war openly against God; enraged against Him because of His great bountifulness to man, but avenging himself on man because he is powerless against God. We see these very qualities in Cain, the first disciple of the devil, who taught him envy and murder.

The firstborn Cain and his younger brother Abel both offered worship to God, but when Cain saw that "the Lord had respect to Abel and to his offerings," whereas to him "and his offerings he had no respect ... Cain was exceedingly angry and his countenance fell."

St. Basil continues:

> What was it Cain did? He saw another honored by God, and burned with envy. He killed the one who was honored, that he might insult Him who honored him. Since he could not attack God, he turned his hatred to the murder of his own brother.

Charity rejoices in goodness wherever it is found, but not so envy, which admires virtue only in itself and is always competing with others for no other reason than its own preferment. Envy is particularly contrary to reason, for there is no way that anyone can take the place prepared by God for each of us individually in heaven. Helping one another grow in virtue only increases it in ourselves.

As God said to Cain, "Why art thou angry? And why is thy countenance fallen? If thou do well, shalt thou not receive? But if ill, shall not sin be present at the door? But the lust thereof shall be under thee, and thou shalt have dominion over it." In other words, it is not the good in others, but the evil in ourselves which creates envy and its consequences, which, for good or ill, always lie within our control.

Says St. Basil:

> Nothing more destructive springs up in the souls of men than the passion of envy, which, while it does no harm to others, is the dominant and peculiar evil of the soul that harbors it. As rust consumes iron, so does envy wholly consume the soul it dwells in.

Perhaps worst of all, "Those not known are not envied, but those with whom we are familiar; and among these again, it arises between persons of the same age, the same kinship, among brothers," and "the more it is aroused, the more bitter it is to the one it masters." As we know, "Cain rose up against his brother Abel and slew him," just as centuries later the Incarnate God himself would be put to death by the chief priests of the Jews "who had delivered him up out of envy" on charges trumped up for the Roman authorities (Gen. 4:3-8; Mk. 15:10).

St. John of the Cross who, unlike the Desert Fathers, makes no capital sin of vanity, regards envy in spiritual form as a root cause of dangerous imperfections in beginners. If he says little about it compared with the other sins, it is only because, as he admits, he is impatient to get to the "nights," which are his main concern. Writing more as the experienced spiritual director than a moral theologian, he has been at pains to show how chameleon-like sins can be and how deeply concealed in human psychology. At this point there is little need to enter into superfluous detail, for the same general principles laid down regarding the preceding sins can be applied easily enough to any others.

He assumes we know that envy, like anger, is both a sin and a passion. Given our fallen nature, the passion of envy arises without our volition and is felt bodily as an anguished contraction of the heart occasioned by seeing the good of others. Common speech calls this experience the "pang of envy." If it is properly controlled and goes no further, it is not only perfectly innocent of any wrongdoing, but can actually benefit the sufferer by leading him to emulate the good he sees. St. John says that

this is indeed the case after God has immersed him in the dark
night of privation. When that happens:

> If the soul has any envy, this is no longer a vice as it was
> before, when it was grieved because others were preferred to it and
> given greater advantage. Its grief now comes from seeing how
> great is its own misery, and its envy, if it has any, is a virtuous
> envy, since it desires to imitate others, which is a great virtue.

The sin of envy, the proverbial "green-eyed monster," is
another matter. It consists in considering the good of others as an
affront to ourselves, as if it detracted in some way from ours.
Envy is not jealousy, although the two are related and often
confused. Jealousy is more akin to avarice, because it consists in
guarding inordinately what is rightfully ours, whereas envy is
directed to what belongs to another. Directly contrary to the
Commandment "Thou shalt not covet," it is mortal in that it
destroys charity. This is particularly true of envy in spiritual
form. St. Thomas says, "To make envy bear upon the spiritual
good of the neighbor is a very grave sin," because these are the
highest goods which can be possessed in this world. Needless to
say, such goods include not only virtues, but answers to prayer, a
fruitful apostolate, visions, locutions or any other special marks
of God's favor.

Envy not only breeds hatred, as it did in Cain, but sows
discord as it did among Jacob's sons, who envied their young
brother Joseph. Even the Apostles had to be rebuked for arguing
among themselves as to which of them was the greatest. The
worldly Pilate easily identified envy as the mainspring of our
Lord's Passion, which otherwise would be unexplainable.
Motivated not only by their own envy, the Pharisees who
orchestrated the deicide were first and foremost the earthly,
visible tools of those fallen spirits on high who goaded them,
inspiring every sadistic detail of the crime.

On the individual level, envy of any kind always destroys
peace of soul, but spiritual envy is more damaging. St. John
notes two symptoms by which it reveals itself, and they are
normally inseparable. The first is a dislike of hearing others

praised for their progress in virtue, and the other is gainsaying whatever good is said of them. The spiritually envious:

> ...are wont to experience movements of displeasure at the spiritual good of others, which cause them a certain sensible grief at being outstripped on the road, so that they would prefer not to hear others praised; for they become displeased at others' virtues and sometimes cannot refrain from contradicting what is said in praise of them, depreciating it as far as they can; and their annoyance thereat grows because the same is not said of them, for they would fain be preferred in everything.

Alas, concludes the mystical doctor:

> All this is clean contrary to charity, which, as St. Paul says, rejoices in goodness. And if charity has any envy, it is a holy envy, comprising grief at not having the virtues of others, yet also joy because others have them, and delight when others outstrip us in the service of God, wherein we ourselves are so remiss.

How to reach such heights? The only remedy is our Lord's: "Go, sit down at the lowest place." In the spiritual life, there's always room at the bottom, and "he that humbleth himself shall be exalted" (Luke 14:10-11).

St. John terminates his list of sins in spiritual guise with one which, like envy, has no place in that of the Desert Fathers, for whom it figures primarily as a component of acedia. It is that mortal laziness called...

Sloth

St. John begins speaking of spiritual sloth by saying, "Beginners are apt to be irked by the things that are most spiritual, from which they flee because these things are incompatible with sensible pleasure." Thus sloth enjoys a natural kinship with lust and gluttony, and like them it makes use of a multitude of disguises. Its effects are far more extensive, however, for intrinsically it is a disease of the will which constantly inclines its victim to avoid any exertion above the ordinary. Always taking the line of least resistance, it avoids the Cross by instinct. This being the case, when the going gets tough and the tough get going in the spiritual life, as happens wherever progress is made, the slothful will give up entirely unless their complaint is brought under control in time.

Hear our Carmelite guide:

> If once they failed to find in prayer the satisfaction which their taste required (and after all it is well that God should take it from them to prove them), they would prefer not to return to it. Sometimes they leave it; at other times they continue it unwillingly. And thus because of this sloth they abandon the way of perfection (which is the way of negation of their will and pleasure for God's sake) for the pleasure and sweetness of their own will, which they aim at satisfying in this way rather than the will of God.

Anyone tempted to relegate sloth among the lesser sins would do well to read in the Gospel how our first Pope fell prey to it. On hearing our Lord say "that he must go to Jerusalem and suffer many things from the ancients and scribes and chief priests and be put to death ... Peter taking him, began to rebuke him, saying, Lord, be it far from thee, this shall not be unto thee!" Thus benevolently counseled to take the sensible way out, our Lord exposed Peter's suggestion as nothing less than satanic. His exact words: "Go behind me, Satan, thou art a scandal unto me, because thou savorest not the things that are of God, but the things that are of men! ... If any man will come after me, let him deny himself and take up his cross and follow me!"

Heavy effort pays off, for the Father will "render to every man according to his works"(Matt. 16:21-27). Referring to this passage in Scripture, St. John explains that those who shun the irksome "are very weak for the fortitude and trial of perfection. They resemble those who are softly nurtured and who run fretfully away from everything that is hard, and take offense at the Cross, wherein consist the delights of the spirit." Taking the easy way may be sloth's most easily recognized characteristic, but as our Lord made clear, in essence it is something more. To be slothful is not the same thing as being phlegmatic. Although sloth seeks repose and relaxation in every endeavor, it doesn't avoid labor *per se* so much as labor it doesn't like. Its goal is not total inertia.

As seen in the Desert Fathers' treatment of boredom and gluttony, very lazy people can appear busy and energetic as long as they are doing what they please, much the same way that the worst gluttons can appear abstemious as long as they eat exactly what they want when they want it. Nor does the malice of sloth lie in doing nothing, which is extremely difficult for most people and often requires considerable will power to endure for any length of time. Sitting dryly before the Blessed Sacrament for an hour's adoration can be very much harder at times than doing a chore requiring physical effort. By the same token a lazy man may pass for a soul of deep prayer because he finds the same time easy and consoling.

On the whole, the preferred diet of the slothful is constant, non-taxing, pleasurable activity. Because sloth is a disease of the will, its precise malice lies in a deadly opposition of its own will to God's.

Says St. John:

> And many of these people would have God will that which they themselves will, and are fretful at having to will that which He wills, and find it repugnant to accommodate their will to that of God. Hence it happens to them that oftentimes they think that that wherein they find not their own will and pleasure is not the will of God; and that, on the other hand, when they themselves find satisfaction, God is satisfied.
>
> Thus they measure God by themselves and not themselves by God, acting quite contrarily to that which He himself taught in the Gospel, saying, that he who should lose his will for His sake, the same should gain it; and he who should desire to gain it, the same should lose it. [Seeking] to go about spiritual matters with complete freedom and according to the inclination of their will, it causes them great sorrow and repugnance to enter upon the narrow way, which, says Christ, is the way of life.

St. John brings his list of spiritual sins to a close by saying that the imperfections he has described are only a sampling "among the many to be found in the lives of those that are in this first state of beginners." He hopes, however, that these goody-goodies as it were, will realize from what he has said, "how greatly they need God to set them in the state of proficients," for no matter how "assiduously the beginner practices the mortification in himself of all these actions and passions of his, he can never completely succeed—very far from it—until God shall work it in him passively by means of the purgation of the said night" of trials and tribulations, both interior and exterior. Try as we will, only God can make saints.

The Deadly Desires

The capital sins cannot be dismissed without a word or two regarding the mysterious "said night," which St. John of the Cross says the beginner must enter if he is to reach perfection. It is the indispensable means employed by God to dry up those deep seated evil inclinations in the soul which will not yield to our own unaided efforts, but which nonetheless requires our active cooperation if it is to succeed. As we know, the wish is father to the deed, and if sin is to be eliminated, it is not enough to cut away what can be seen above ground. What lies underneath and out of sight must be excised. As St. John the Baptist said, the axe must be laid to the root of the trees.

Masters of the spiritual life all warn those under their direction to watch for sin in its small, apparently innocuous beginnings. The camel, they say, has only to get his nose under the tent to pull the whole thing down, and once the serpent finds an opening large enough for his head, the whole length of his body quickly follows. The Incarnate Truth himself told us that anyone who curses his brother is already a murderer and that a man who looks upon a woman with lust has committed adultery with her in his heart.

The literal-minded find Psalm 136 hard to explain in the light of Christian charity, where it addresses Babylon in no uncertain terms, crying out "Blessed be he that shall take and dash thy little ones against the rock!" but the true meaning is clear. Far from sanctioning infanticide, Scripture is telling us that evil must be ruthlessly destroyed before it reaches maturity, when it is still relatively helpless against us and can be dealt with. And the rock, of course, is Christ.

St. John of the Cross therefore expounds the "nights" in terms of the mortification or purgation of the desires, first as to sense, and then as to spirit. Whereas the Desert Fathers explore the psychology of sin-as-it-happens, the Carmelite master might be said to expose the ramifications of sin-before-it-happens. Because sin first exists in desire before coming to fruition, he devotes the first of the three parts of *The Ascent of Mt. Carmel* to the baneful role played by all too human cravings in the life of prayer, and how they must be gradually extinguished by God's action.

> He does this by bringing them into the dark night ... wherein He weans them from the breasts of these sweetnesses and pleasures, gives them pure aridities and inward darkness, takes from them all these irrelevances and puerilities, and by very different means causes them to win the virtues.

Whether or not the soul is able to follow God's lead at this point and learn to do without consolation marks a crucial stage, for what is actually an indication of His growing interest in us, is usually interpreted by the inexperienced as sure proof of His absence. Painful deprivation, however, is the normal preparation for great graces.

In Exodus, just before God gives Moses the tablets of the Law, He tells him:

> Be ready by morning, and come up to the mountains of Sinai at dawn; await my orders there at the top of the mountain. No one must come up with you, no one be seen anywhere on the mountain; even the flocks and herds may not graze in front of this mountain.

Expounding this text, St. John says that anyone who expects to commune with God must renounce everything and leave it below. Not even our desires, legitimate as they may be, which are represented by the beasts in the story, must be allowed to feed in the vicinity.

Is our Lord to be believed or not when He says, "If any man come to me and hate not his father and mother and wife and children and brethren and sisters, yea, and his own life also, he cannot be my disciple ... Everyone of you that doth not renounce all that he possesseth, cannot be my disciple?" Before embarking on the spiritual life, let him "first sit down and reckon the charges that are necessary ... lest .. he is not able to finish" (Luke 14:26-29,33).

Fallen nature has an innate tendency to Manichaeanism, looking for sin in things rather than in ourselves. We prefer to think that alcoholism is caused by alcohol, that a strict diet is insurance against gluttony, that staying away from those sexually attractive to us will make us pure, etc. Avoiding occasions of sin is essential, but only when joined to the realization that sinfulness always springs from the *fomes peccati* in our own fallen human nature, that ever present tinder that only needs a spark to set it ablaze.

In other words, it is impossible to become holy by giving up desserts, sex, tobacco, designer clothes, tickets to the ball games or anything else, without first giving up the desire for such things. Only when the desire is relinquished, do they present no danger. No evil in the world can harm us if we have no desire for it. It might as well not exist. As St. Paul wrote to Titus, the young Bishop of Crete, "All things are clean to the clean, but to them that are defiled, and to unbelievers, nothing is clean: but both their mind and their conscience are defiled." (Titus 1:15)

A major source of St. John of the Cross' doctrine, St. Paul also said, "The desire of money is the root of all evils." Saying money is the root of all evil, as commonly heard, not only seriously misquotes Scripture, but propagates the error of the Manichees. As our Lord taught in the parable of the unjust steward, the mammon of iniquity can be set to good purposes, having no power of its own to hurt anyone. It is only those who love it who "fall into temptation and into the snare of the devil and into many unprofitable and hurtful desires, which drown men into destruction and perdition. For the desire of money is the root of all evils; which some coveting have erred from the faith, and have entangled themselves in many sorrows." (1 Tim. 6:10) .

There are two principal reasons why our disordered wants constitute a danger for us. One is privative and the other positive, but the first far outweighs the other: Desires deprive us of God by leaving us no room for Him. To read St. John on this subject today, in the light of all the post-conciliar nonsense about "togetherness" and "building community," finding God in other people, is like a refreshing plunge into cool water. Speaking authoritatively as a Doctor of the Church, in the precise language of the trained theologian, he explains the matter without subterfuge:

> It is clear from the very fact that when the soul becomes affectioned to a thing which comes under the head of a creature, that the more the desire for that thing fills the soul, the less capacity has the soul for God. Inasmuch as two contraries ... cannot co-exist in one person, since ... affection for God and affection for creatures are contraries, there cannot be contained within one will affection for creatures and affection for God. For what has the creature to do with the Creator? The sensual to do with the spiritual? Visible with invisible? Temporal with eternal?... Christ-like poverty of spirit with attachment to anything?

Sooner or later, a choice must be made.

The second reason that desires are dangerous is that, of themselves, desires are actually noxious. Besides crowding out God, they cause positive harm in five specific ways:

1. They *weary* us, tiring us beyond endurance, "like restless and discontented children who are ever demanding this or that from their mother and are never contented." The more we try to quell our cravings by giving in to them, the more insatiable they become, for "desire is like fire, which increases as wood is thrown upon it." God never created us to find satisfaction in creatures. Only He can satisfy us, and catering to a thousand wants leaves no time for God at all. As He lamented through His prophet Jeremias, "My people ... have forsaken me, the fountain of living water, and have digged to themselves ... broken cisterns, that can hold no water" (Jer. 2: 13).

2. Desires actively *torment* us. They make us suffer and writhe as if we were tied up with tight ropes, never giving us a moment's freedom.

> Even as one that lies naked upon thorns and briars is tormented and afflicted, even so is the soul tormented and afflicted when it rests upon its desires ... And even as the husbandman, coveting the harvest for which he hopes, afflicts and torments the ox in the plough, even so does concupiscence afflict a soul that is subject to its desire to attain that for which it longs.

Needless to say, the stronger the desire, the greater the oppression.

3. Desires *blind* us, darkening the soul to the point of obliterating our spiritual vision. The effect on the prayer life of modern society's perpetual solicitations to power and possession, generating artificial needs and ambitions of every kind, is too evident to require comment, but St. John says that even our natural reason is unable to operate properly when the desires are excited. He also notes:

> At this same time, when the soul is darkened in the understanding, it is also benumbed in the will, and the memory becomes dull and disordered ... for, as these faculties depend on the understanding, it is clear that when the understanding is impeded, they (too) will become disordered and troubled.

He explains that desire itself is blind, "since of itself it has no understanding ... the reason being to it always, as it were, a child leading a blind man. And hence ... when the soul is guided by its desire, it becomes blind. And, as our Lord said, 'If the blind lead the blind, both fall into the pit'" (Matt. 15:14).

4. Desire *stains* the soul. Scripture says, "He that toucheth pitch shall be defiled with it" (Ecclus. 13:1), and the saint explains:

> A man touches pitch when he allows the desire of his will to be satisfied by any creature ... for there is more difference between excellence of soul and the best of creatures than there is between

pure diamond, or fine gold, and pitch ... A single unruly desire, although there be in it no matter of mortal sin, suffices to bring a soul into such bondage, foulness and vileness that it can in no wise come to accord with God in union until the desire be purified. What then will be the vileness of the soul that is completely unrestrained with respect to its own passions and given up to its desires, and how far removed will it be from God and from His purity?

In Ezechiel can be found an inspired description of disordered human desires and the way they defile God's temple, which every baptized soul is meant to be. Ordered by an angelic messenger to dig through the wall to look inside, the prophet sees that "every form of creeping things and of living creatures, the abomination, and all the idols of the house of Israel were painted on the wall round about," and that incense was being offered to them (Ez. 8:7-11).

5. Finally, desires *weaken* us, making us lukewarm in the service of God and the pursuit of virtue. The words of our Lord concerning the tribulations of the last days, "Woe to them that are with child and that give suck" (Matt. 24:19), St. John interprets to mean those sapped of strength by their desires.

> If they be not pruned will ever be taking more virtue from the soul and will grow to the harm of the soul, like the shoots upon the tree ... They are also like leeches which are ever sucking the blood from the veins ... Just so the desires that are not mortified grow to such a point that they kill the soul with respect to God because it has not first killed them ... It is very piteous to consider ... For there is no evil humor that makes it as wearisome and difficult for a sick man to walk, or gives him a distaste for eating comparable to the weariness and distaste for following virtue which is given to a soul by desire for creatures.

All in all, St. John seems to paint a very discouraging picture, but he goes on to reassure us that no natural desire can hurt us unless it is voluntary and habitually consented to. If they never pass beyond first movements, they harm us no more than involuntary distractions in prayer. Our task is to support God's action in our regard and see to it that they remain unconsented to.

> One must greatly lament the ignorance of certain men who burden themselves with extraordinary penances and with many other voluntary practices, and think that this practice or that will be sufficient to bring them to the union of Divine Wisdom; but such will not be the case if they endeavor not diligently to mortify their desires.

Safety lies in never giving way to mere feelings or self will. Among the seventy-six admonitions the saint left behind in his own hand is found one reading:

> That man will not be able to attain perfection who endeavors not to be satisfied with nothing, so that his natural and spiritual concupiscence may be content with emptiness; for this is needful if a man would attain to the highest tranquility and peace of spirit; and in this way the love of God is almost continually in action in the simple and pure soul.

To an inquirer who wanted to know what methods to use to reach ecstasy, he replied, *"By renouncing one's own will and doing the will of God!* For ecstasy is naught but the going forth of a soul from itself and its being caught up in God, and this is what happens to the soul that is obedient, namely, that it goes forth from itself and from its own desires, and thus lightened of its load, becomes immersed in God." (points of Love, 65)

Writing from Segovia to one of his spiritual sons in religion, St. John said:

> The desire is the mouth of the will, which opens wide when it is not impeded or filled with any morsel, that is, with any pleasure; for when the desire is set upon anything, it becomes constrained, and apart from God, everything is constraint.

On his famous illustration of the ascent of the Mount of Perfection can be read the following lines summing up his doctrine on the desires:

In order to arrive at having pleasure in everything, Desire to have pleasure in nothing.

In order to arrive at possessing everything, Desire to possess nothing.

In order to arrive at being everything, Desire to be nothing.

In order to arrive at knowing everything, Desire to know nothing.

In order to arrive at that wherein thou hast no pleasure, Thou must go by a way wherein thou hast no pleasure.

In order to arrive at that which thou knowest not, Thou must go by a way that thou knowest not.

In order to arrive at that which thou possessest not, Thou must go by a way thou possessest not.

In order to arrive at that which thou art not, Thou must go through that which thou art not.

Or, as our Lord put it, "He that will save his life shall lose it, and he that shall lose his life for my sake shall find it!" (Matt 16:25).

The Devil Revisited

No one was more aware than St. John of the Cross of the role played by the devil in the spiritual life, whose machinations bring out the best in the good and the worst in the others. In the "Cautions" which he drew up for the nuns he directed in Beas, he said that of those three implacable enemies which every soul encounters in this life—the world, the flesh and the devil—the world is the most easily dealt with. The world, after all, exists outside us and can be largely ignored, even abandoned entirely if necessary. The flesh he calls "the most tenacious of all," because, alas, it is part of our nature, and as the Desert Fathers also taught, it continues to assault us to the bitter end.

Unfortunately, "In order to conquer anyone of these three enemies, it is necessary to conquer them all three," but on the other hand, "if one is weakened, the other two are weakened; and when all three are conquered, no more war remains in the soul." Of the three, the devil is a most formidable opponent, being "the hardest to understand." He cannot be outwitted, for human intelligence is not equal to his. In the final clinches only supernatural obedience can match his stratagems, for it lies above reason and is completely beyond his comprehension.

The first thing novices in the spiritual life should know about him is that he will try to deceive them "under an appearance of what is good and not under an appearance of what is evil, for he knows that if they recognize evil they will hardly touch it." This is the ordinary gambit of the "noonday devil" so rightly feared by the Desert Fathers. St. John said, "In order to deceive the soul and to instill falsehoods into it, the devil first feeds it with truths and things that are probable in order to give it assurance and afterwards to deceive it." He compares him to "one that sews leather with a bristle, first piercing the leather with the sharp bristle, after which enters the soft thread; the thread could not enter unless the bristle guided it." Thus healthy "misgivings concerning that which seems good," are necessary at all times.

To those seriously intending to battle the powers of hell, St. John offers three cautions. These were formulated for religious, but due proportion kept, they apply as well to laymen who, while not under vows, are nonetheless bound to perform their duties of state and obey the orders of legitimate superiors:

1. The first is never to withdraw from due obedience. Always avoiding attachments of any kind, be "moved to nothing, however good and full of charity it may seem, whether it be for yourself or anyone within or without the house," which is not sanctioned by proper authority. "And if you do not observe this caution, both in little things and great, however successful you seem to be, you cannot fail, either to a small or to a great degree, to be deceived by the devil."

2. "Never consider your superior as less than if he were God, be the superior who he may, for to you he stands in the place of God." Especially avoid,

> ...with great vigilance from considering his character, his ways or his habits or any of his other characteristics, for if you do this, you will do yourself the harm of exchanging divine obedience for human, by being moved or unmoved only by the visible characteristics of your superior, instead of by the invisible God whom you serve in his person.

This applies equally to superiors we like or dislike, for,

> ...your obedience will be vain, or will be the more unfruitful, if you take offense at any unpleasing characteristic in your superior, or rejoice when you find him good or pleasant. For I tell you, the devil has ruined the perfection of a great multitude ... by causing them to consider these characteristics.

Unless you learn to disregard your personal feelings, "you can in no wise become a spiritual person."

3. Finally, "Strive ever to humble your heart in word and deed, rejoicing in the good of others as at your own, and desiring that others be preferred to yourself in all things, and this with all

your heart." It may not seem so, but this caution is "aimed directly against the devil." Not only is it a way of overcoming evil with good, but "you will cast the devil far from you and will have joy of heart. " And by way of icing on the cake, St. John adds, "Try to practice this most with respect to those who least attract you ... and love ever to be taught by all men rather than to desire to teach him that is least of all."

In the course of expounding his doctrine on the mystical life, St. John acquaints us with many of the stratagems used by our common enemy in his war against us. Temptations to the capital sins, in both carnal and spiritual form are the devil's stock in trade, but as the soul progresses in virtue and union with God, his strategy tends to become more subtle. A master of deception, he excels in counterfeiting visions, locutions and other supernatural communications, making easy prey of those desiring such things:

> The devil causes many to believe in vain visions and false prophecies, and strives to make them presume that God and the saints are speaking with them; and they often trust their own fancy. And the devil is also accustomed to fill them with presumption and pride, so that they become attracted by vanity and arrogance and allow themselves to be seen engaging in outward acts which appear holy, such as raptures and other manifestations. ... It is very doubtful if such souls will return to the pure road of virtue and spirituality.

Although he is a spirit, the devil is irremediably cut off from the life of grace. Having no means of discerning the supernatural, he is severely limited in both knowledge and power, incapable of penetrating the inner sanctuary of the human soul or reading its inmost thoughts. This being the case, he "takes his stand, with great cunning, on the road which leads from sense to spirit, deceiving and luring the soul by means of sense and giving it sensual things." Aware from outward indications that the soul already detached from creatures is coming closer to God, "he has heavy grief and envy," seeing that it is "flying beyond him and he can in no wise lay hold on it."

Unable to subvert it by appeals to sense, he may flood it:

> ...with cataracts of knowledge and mists of sweetness, which are sometimes good, so that he may ... cause it to return to a different way of life and to the operation of sense, and to look at these delights and this good knowledge which he sets before it, and embrace them, so that it may continue its journey to God in reliance upon them.

Through the power of suggestion "he can represent to the soul many kinds of intellectual knowledge and implant them so firmly that it appears impossible that they should not be true," causing his victim "to believe innumerable falsehoods if it be not humble and cautious." If it be lacking in obedience to proper authority, this is all the more likely. Given the weakness of human nature, diabolic suggestion can cause knowledge "to sink into the soul with such great power, persuasiveness and determination that the soul needs to give itself earnestly to prayer and to exert great strength if it is to cast it off."

These lines make it easy to guess, not only how heresies are implanted in the Church, but how delusions masquerading as mental disease can be introduced into the minds of individuals. What better description of some all too common symptoms of paranoia than the following:

> At times the devil is accustomed to represent to the soul the sins of others, and evil consciences and evil *souls, falsely but very vividly* and all this he does to harm the soul, trusting that it may spread abroad his revelations and that thus more sins may be committed, for which reason he fills the soul with zeal by making it believe that these revelations are granted it so that it may commend the persons to God.

Although God does sometimes grant such revelations, "it is more often the devil ... in order to cause infamy, sin and discouragement, whereof," says St. John, "we have very great experience." Among his maxims is found the following: "Never take man for an example in that which you have to do, howsoever holy he be, for else the devil will set his imperfections before you. But imitate Christ, who is the sum of perfection and the sum of holiness, and you shall never go astray."

Warning of the dangers lurking in the apostolate for the unmortified, he points out that another diabolic ploy is to inspire works which may be good in themselves, but which are not intended by God, or not intended at that particular time. "For when the devil sees them affectioned to these things, he opens a wide field to them, gives them abundant material and interferes with them in many ways; whereupon they spread their sails and become shamelessly audacious in the freedom wherewith they work these marvels." They may even become "bold enough to work with him by an explicit and manifest compact ... as his disciples and allies. Hence we have wizards, enchanters, magicians, soothsayers and sorcerers."

Delighting most in bringing down souls far advanced in the spiritual life, the devil is especially envious of anyone on the threshold of divine union. In *The Spiritual Canticle,* St. John explains how he

> ...contrives to set horror and fear in its spirit. ... sometimes he even threatens it within its very spirit. And when he sees that he cannot reach the inmost part of the soul, since it is deeply recollected and closely united to God, he then attacks it from without, in its sensual part, and sets distraction or inconstancy and sensible afflictions and pains and horror, if haply by this means he may harry the Bride in her marriage-chamber. (XXIX and XXX, 6).

All in all, "there is hardly any soul walking on this road which does not meet with great injuries and suffer great losses."

Mystical progress to union with God being the Carmelite Doctor's main concern, he left behind no systematized demonology. Information of this kind must therefore be mined from the body of his works, through which it runs like a tantalizing vein of gold. Apart from the nuggets offered above, a detailed summary of his teaching on the demonic far exceeds the competence of this opusculum, which is content to close with two items culled from the the saint's axioms which sum up all we really need to know about the devil. The first is, "The soul that is united with God is feared by the devil as though it were God himself." And like unto it is the second, which says, "He that trusts to himself is worse than the devil!"

Cui bono? What's the use? Who would head for the spiritual heights in the Age of Apostasy? Father Elias, mighty in word and deed, who had raised a dead child to life and put to death the priests of Baal after making fools of them in public, was not immune to similar discouragement. Fleeing the wrath of Jezebel, he "went forward one day's journey into the desert. And when he was there and sat under a juniper tree, he requested for his soul that he might die." He concluded, "I am no better than my fathers. And he cast himself down and slept in the shadow of the juniper tree" so weary was he of the sins of Israel.

Miraculously fed by an angel, he takes refuge in a cave on Mt. Horeb, where God finds him and asks, "What dost thou here, Elias?" And the prophet answers, "The children of Israel have forsaken thy covenant. They have thrown down thy altars, they have slain thy prophets with the sword, and I alone am left, and they seek my life to take it away," convinced that he had done all he could in the face of such massive defection. But God tells him not to be misled by appearances, for "I will leave me seven thousand men in Israel, whose knees have not bowed before Baal!"

Commenting on this passage at the height of the Arian heresy, St. John Chrysostom assured his beleaguered congregation that many people unknown to them continued to observe God's commands in spite of everything.

> If we do not believe this, it is not because there are none who live holy lives, but because we are ourselves far from doing this.

Just as a drunkard will not readily believe there are persons who do not drink even water; ... nor will he who has sinned with countless women readily believe virginity is possible; nor will he who robs others believe that anyone of his own choice would give up what is his own; nor will they who are consumed all day by anxieties readily accept this teaching.

He concluded:

That there are many who have come to this perfection we could show you ... but we shall be satisfied with you if you give alms plentifully; for if we do this we shall soon go on to higher things. Therefore, keeping before our mind those degrees of self discipline which have been set before us, let us strive to attain at least to those midway on the road, so that we may be delivered from the wrath to come and, drawing ever nearer, may come at last to the very crown of all blessings.

The beginner begins where he is, and if he perseveres, God in due time will introduce him into the "nights" of purgation of sense and spirit reserved for the stalwart. St. Augustine said the devil makes a point of circulating evil about good people "that the weak may then think there are not any good, and so let themselves be carried away by their own evil desires and become corrupted, saying to themselves, Who is there keeps a commandment of God? Or who observes chastity? And when a man believes that no one does, he himself becomes that 'no one.'"

In his prologue to *The Ascent of Mt. Carmel,* St. John of the Cross admitted that it was never his "principal intent to address all," but rather those "to whom God is granting the favor of setting on the road ..." What's more, in *The Dark Night of the Soul* he promises they will:

...suffer great trials, by reason not so much of the aridities which they suffer, as of the fear which they have of being lost on the road, thinking that all spiritual blessing is over for them and that God has abandoned them since they find no help or pleasure in good things.

What better description of the purgative night Mother Church herself is now undergoing in those members who truly love God and will not bow the knee to Baal? Needless to say, shortly before the opening of the fateful Council which launched the tribulation, the mighty voice of Elias, ever faithful to his mission, sounded the alarm from the Carmel of Coimbra, Portugal. On September 26, 1957, a true daughter of his, Sr. Lucy of Fatima, told the Mexican priest Fr. Augustine Fuentes in what may have been her last contact with the outside:

> Father, we should not wait for an appeal to the world to come from Rome on the part of the Holy Father to do penance. Nor should we wait for the call to do penance to come from our bishops in our dioceses, nor from the religious congregations. No! Our Lord has already very often used these means, and the world has not paid attention. That is why now it is necessary for each one of us to reform ourselves spiritually. Each person must not only save his own soul, but also all the souls that God has placed in our path!

Or, as Elias himself put it to the wavering Israelites on the Mount, "How long do you halt between two sides? If the Lord be God, follow him: But if Baal, then follow him!"(3Kgs.18:21)

Saint Elias, living still,
Lead us upward, if you will!

Bibliography

John Cassian, *Institutes*, Books I_V, VII-XII; *Conferences*, Book V, "The Eight Principal Faults;" Book XVI, "On Friendships," *The Nicene and Post Nicene Fathers*, Vol. XI, Second Series, Wm. B Eerdsman Publishing Co., Grand Rapids, Michigan, 1964.

Jean Cassien, *Institutions Cénobitiques*, Livre VI, "De l'Esprit de Fornication," Editions du Cerf, Paris, 1965.

Jean Cassien, *Conférences*, Vol. II, "De la Chasteté," Editions du Cerf, Paris, 1958.

St. John of the Cross, *Complete Works*. E. Allison Peers translation, Newman Press, Westminster, Maryland, 1953.

Sunday Sermons of the Great Fathers, ed. M.F. Toal, D.D., Henry Regnery Co., Chicago, 1963.

Helen Waddell, *The Desert Fathers*, Ann Arbor Books, University of Michigan Press, Ann Arbor, Michigan, 1957.

Quotations from Sacred Scripture are taken from the Rheims-Douai translation of the Vulgate.